# PEARLS OF WISDOM

SWAMI VIVEKANANDA

### THE RAMAKRISHNA MISSION
### INSTITUTE OF CULTURE
GOL PARK, KOLKATA 700 029

*Published by*
Swami Sarvabhutananda, Secretary
Ramakrishna Mission Institute of Culture
Gol Park, Kolkata-700 029, India

**First Edition** : January 1988 : 3,000
Thirteenth Impression : June 2009 : 11,000
Total Impression : 1,31,000

**Published on the occasion of the
125th birth anniversary of Swami Vivekananda**

**ISBN** : 81-85843-24-4

**Price** : Rupees Thirty-five only

*Printed in India*

Computer typeset at
Ramakrishna Mission Institute of Culture
Koplkata 700 029

Photo-offset at

Trio Process
Kolkata 700 014

# Foreword

Unawares, Swami Vivekananda very often said things that startled his audience. He said them casually, carelessly, without any thought about the impact that they might produce. What he said might be simple truths, but it is these simple truths, spoken with authority and coming spontaneously from a world teacher, that disturb you most. They remind you of your present limitations and of the great heights to which you might yet rise. They shake you to your roots, sweeping away all the depression you have allowed to accumulate over the years and releasing within you new sources of energy which carry you forward.

It is some of such utterances by Swami Vivekananda which Prof. Govinda Gopal Mukhopadhyaya, with the assistance of two research assistants, working under him, Madhabi Sinha and Parna Mukherjee, has picked up from among Swamiji's speeches and writings from *The Complete Works of Swami Vivekananda* published by Advaita Ashrama, Mayavati, which this little book presents to the readers. While reading the utterances the readers may experience the same kind of electric shock which Romain Rolland experienced when he first read Swamiji.

1 January 1988          Swami Lokeswarananda

At the Parliament of Religions : September 1893

## Abnegation (*Sadhana*)

Abnegation has the greatest importance in our philosophy. Negation implies affirmation of the Real Self. The Vedanta is pessimistic so far as it negatives the world of the senses, but it is optimistic in its assertion of the real world. (V. 283)

## Absolute

The Absolute does not change, or re-evolve. (I. 420)

Changes in the universe are not in the Absolute; they are in nature. (I. 420)

There is a joy which is Absolute, which never changes. (II. 167)

In the Absolute, there is neither time, space, nor causation; It is all one. (II. 132)

If the Absolute becomes limited by the mind, it is no more Absolute. (II. 132)

The Absolute cannot be divided. (III. 7)

The Absolute does not come within Maya. (V. 310)

The Absolute can never be thought of. (VI. 108)

Only when creation stops can we find the Absolute. The Absolute is in the Soul, not in creation. (VI. 96)

The Absolute cannot be worshipped, so we must worship a manifestation. (VII. 29)

The sea calm is the Absolute; the same sea in waves is Divine Mother. (VII. 27)

The Absolute God of the universe, the creator, preserver, and destroyer of the universe, is impersonal principle. (VIII. 133-34)

The Absolute is the material of both God and man. (VIII. 179)

## Achievement

Every great achievement is done slowly. (VI. 332)

## Advaita

Nothing gives such strength as this idea of monism. Nothing makes us so moral as this idea of monism. (II. 201)

Monism and dualism are essentially the same. (VI. 98)

Monism, or absolute oneness is the very soul of Vedanta. (VII. 28)

## Argument

All argument and reasoning must be based upon certain perceptions. (II. 162)

## Art

Art is—representing the beautiful. There must be Art in everything. (V. 259)

Art must be in touch with nature—and wherever that touch is gone, Art degenerates—yet it (Art) must be above nature. (V. 258)

## Atheists

We are all atheists; let us confess it. Mere intellectual assent does not make us religious. (II. 164)

A man who does not believe in himself is an atheist. (II. 294)

## Attachment

As soon as we identify ourselves with the work we do, we feel miserable. (I. 100)

Attachment comes only where we expect a return. (I. 59)

Everything that you do under compulsion goes to build up attachment. (I. 104)

All misery and pain come from attachment. (II. 392)

It is attachment, identification, which makes us miserable. (II. 37)

There is only one attachment and that belongs to the Lord, and to none other. (IV. 96)

Our misery comes, not from work, but by our getting attached to something. (IV. 96)

If you can get rid of your attachment to a single thing, you are on the way to liberation. (VII. 410)

**Attempt**

Even our smallest attempts are not in vain. (II. 36)

In every attempt there will be one set of men who will applaud, and another who will pick holes. (VI. 269)

**Atom**

One atom has the power of the whole universe at its back. (V. 217)

**Attraction**

This mighty attraction in the direction of God makes all other attractions vanish for him (*Bhakti-yogi*). (III. 75)

**Baptism**

Baptism is the direct introduction into the life of the spirit. (VIII. 114)

**Belief**

Belief is no part of religion. We say religion is a superconscious state. (V. 303)

If you believe in a God, you can see Him even now. (II. 372)

Lord ! how hard it is for man to believe in Thee and Thy
    mercies ! (VI. 303)

Whatever you believe, that you will be. (III. 284)

Those who are believers are heroes. (VI. 319)

## Belur Math

The aim of this institution is to make men. (III. 447)

## Bhakta

Wherever there is beauty or sublimity, to him (*Bhakta*)
    it is all His. (III. 76)

He who wants to become a *Bhakta* must be strong, must
    be healthy. (III. 69)

'Everything is His and He is my Lover; I love Him,'
    says the *Bhakta*. (III. 82)

No *Bhakta* cares for anything except love, except to love
    and to be loved. (III. 99)

'In this evanescent world, where everything is falling to
    pieces, we have to make the highest use of what time
    we have,' says the *Bhakta*. (III. 84)

The *Bhakta* in this state of perfect resignation, arising
    out of intense love to God, and to all that are His,
    ceases to distinguish between pleasure and pain in
    so far as they affect him. He does not know what it
    is to complain of pain or misery; and this kind of
    uncomplaining resignation to the will of God, who
    is all love, is indeed a worthier acquisition than all
    the glory of grand and heroic performances. (III. 83)

Through every face shines to him (*Bhakta*) his Hari. (III. 76)

The person who aspires to be a *Bhakta* must be
    cheerful. (III. 69)

The *Bhakta* loves the Lord because He is lovable. (III. 87)

The *Bhakta's* renunciation is that *Vairagya* or non-attachment for all things that are not God which results from *Anuraga* or great attachment to God. (III. 76)

Our allegiance is to the principles always, and not to the persons. (III. 280)

## Bhakti

The great quality of Bhakti is that it cleanses the mind. (III. 358)

Hatred is a thing which greatly impedes the course of Bhakti. (III. 358)

Bhakti can be more easily practised by persons in every condition of life. (III. 357)

'*Pranidhana* is that sort of Bhakti, in which, without seeking results, such as sense-enjoyments etc., all works are dedicated to that Teacher of teachers.' (III. 36)

## Bhakti-Yoga

Bhakti-Yoga is natural, sweet and gentle. (III. 78)

Bhakti-Yoga does not say, 'Give up'; it only says, 'Love, love the Highest !' (III. 74)

## Blow

Blows are what awaken us and help to break the dream. (VII. 79)

## Body

This thirst after body is the great bane of human life. (I. 264)

Body is the name of a series of changes. (I. 142)

Not one body is constant. (I. 151)

This body is a combination. (I. 256)

This idea of body is a simple superstition. (I. 256)

We have to keep the body in good health. (I. 139)

All the forces that are working in this body have been produced out of food. (I. 136)

Body is an unreal dream, and we think we are all bodies. (I. 287)

When the forces that hold it together go away, the body must fall. (I. 142)

The body and mind are dependent. (II. 502)

Bodies come and go, but the soul does not change. (II. 246)

Body is the name of a stream of matter continuously changing. (II. 272)

The body cannot be the soul. (II. 232)

The less the thought of the body, the better. (II. 37)

Here is the greatest of altars, the living, conscious human body. (II. 314)

It is the body that drags us down. (II. 37)

This body is not I; it must go. (III. 11)

It is the want that creates the body. (V. 250)

The body is our enemy, and yet is our friend. (V. 253)

The body is mortal and the mind is mortal; both, being compounds, must die. (VI. 128)

There is but one temple—the body. It is the only temple that ever existed. (VIII. 135)

The body must be properly taken care of. (VI. 130)

Get rid of the bondage of body. (VIII. 18)

Body is our schoolmaster. (VIII. 19)

## Bondage

A golden chain is as much a chain as an iron one. (I. 55; V. 317)

The chain of gold is quite as bad as the chain of
    iron. (I. 500)

Free will is a misnomer. (II. 283)

The ghosts of past thoughts, past lives hold us
    down. (VI. 30)

We think in time; our thoughts are bound by time; all
    that exists, exists in time and space. (VI. 34)

We must learn not only to attach the mind to one thing
    exclusively, but also to detach it at a moment's notice
    and place it upon something else. (VI. 38)

Bondage brings only misery. (VIII. 414)

Desire, ignorance, and inequality—this is the trinity of
    bondage. (VIII. 344)

Our bondage is a delusion. (II. 197)

If you say you are bound, bound you will remain. (II. 350)

He who says he is bound, bound he shall remain.
    (VI. 311)

As long as we require someone else to make us happy,
    we are slaves. (V. 239)

He whose senses rule him is worldly—is a slave. (VIII. 40)

We are all slaves to our senses, slaves to our own minds,
    conscious and subconscious. (VI. 29)

We are all slaves to our own and to everybody else's
    mind. (VI. 29)

We are led here and there because we cannot help
    ourselves. (VI. 29)

We think because we have to think. (VI. 29)

To weep is a sign of weakness, of bondage. (V. 275)

## Book

No book ever created a soul. (I. 324)

Clinging to books only degenerates the human mind. (I. 185)

No amount of books can help us to become purer. (II. 336)

'Books are good but they are only maps.' (II. 503)

No one becomes learned by reading books. (IV. 20)

By reading books we become parrots. (IV. 20)

A book is the most tangible form of God. (IV. 44)

The living power you cannot find in the books. (VIII. 116)

Books cannot teach God, but they can destroy ignorance; their action is negative. (VII. 53)

Mere book-learning won't do. (V. 342)

Mere book-learned Pandits are of no avail. (III. 452)

Book-worship is the worst form of idolatry. (VIII. 34)

## Brahmacharya

Is there a greater strength than that of *Brahmacharya*— Purity, my boy? (VI. 271)

## Brahmin

The Buddhists cannot stand without the brain and philosophy of the Brahmins, nor the Brahmin, without the heart of the Buddhist. (I. 23)

The birth of the Brahmin is 'for the protection of the treasury of religion'. (III. 152)

The plan in India is to make everybody a Brahmin, the Brahmin being the ideal of humanity. (V. 214)

## Brave

The brave are always moral. (V. 3)

The brave alone can afford to be sincere. (VI. 110)

None but the bravest deserves salvation. (I. 479)

The brave alone do great things, not the cowards. (V. 86)

## Causation

Everything that we know, or can possibly know, must be subject to causation. (I. 96)

All law has its essence in causation. (I. 95)

One link in a chain explains the infinite chain. (III. 161)

Everything, both mental and physical, is rigidly bound by the law of causation. (VIII. 145)

Everything has a cause. (VII. 424)

## Cause and Effect

Where no bondage is, there is no cause and effect. (VII. 103)

We are the effects, and we are the causes. (III. 125)

Nothing can be produced without a cause, and the effect is but the cause reproduced. (II. 425)

There cannot be a cause without an effect. (III. 414)

The effect is delusion, and therefore the cause must be delusion. (III. 13)

The cause being finite, the effect must be finite. (II. 17)

The cause of today is the effect of the past and the cause for the future. (IV. 141-42)

The finer is always the cause, the grosser the effect. (I. 132)

The subtle are the causes, the gross the effects. (I. 122)

Cause is the fine state of the manifested state. (II. 442)

Everything is present in its cause, in its fine form. (V. 255)

No effect of work can be eternal. (II. 244)

Something cannot be made out of nothing. (II. 426)

Something cannot come out of nothing. (VI. 157)

Nothing can be created out of nothing. (II. 208)

Nothing comes without a cause. (II. 207)

All virtuous actions bring pleasure, and all vicious actions bring pain. (I. 246)

What one has done one must suffer. (V. 239)

We are in this world by our own actions. (II. 257)

What we are now is the result of our past practice. (IV. 8)

We are the makers of our own fate. (II. 224)

We make our own destiny. (II. 224)

We reap what we sow. (II. 224)

We get only what we deserve. (IV. 301)

No one is to blame for our miseries but ourselves. (I. 342)

With the sense of possession comes selfishness. (I. 100)

Want and anxiety are the causes of all unhappiness and happiness too. (VI. 53)

All the evil acts must produce their results also. (II. 271)

Immorality leads to bondage. (II. 141)

Existence never comes out of non-existence. (I. 297)

The idea of power brings with it awe. (III. 95)

We only get what we deserve. (II. 8)

As soon as the field is ready, the seed must and does come. (III. 46)

Ignorance is the great mother of all misery. (II. 83)

## Chance

Every moment is a new chance. (VII. 425)

## Change

Change is the nature of all objective things. (V. 429)

All change is in the screen. (V. 285)

Change can only be in the limited. (II. 79)

Change is always in regard to something which does not change. (II. 345)

Everybody is changing. (III. 347)

## Character

Character is repeated habits, and repeated habits alone can reform character. (I. 208)

It is character that cleaves its way through adamantine walls of difficulties. (IV. 367)

It is character that pays everywhere. (V. 51)

Upon ages of struggle a character is built. (V. 57)

Perfect love, the heart never reacting, this is what builds character. (VI. 135)

Character has to be established through a thousand stumbles. (VIII. 383)

## Charity

Test everything, try everything, and then believe it, and if you find it for the good of many, give it to all. (III. 528)

There is no higher virtue than charity. (IV. 10)

Charity never faileth. (VI. 121)

The hand was made to give always. (IV. 10)

'For the good of the many, for the happiness of the many' great-souled men take their birth. (IV. 419)

## Chastity

Chastity is the life of a nation. (II. 101)

Chastity is the corner-stone of all morality and of all religion. (VIII. 46)

## Child

It is good to be born a child, but bad to remain a child. (I. 325)

A child teaches itself. (IV. 55)

A child educates itself. (IV. 55)

## Civilization

No civilization can grow unless fanaticism, bloodshed, and brutality stop. (III. 187)

Civilization, true civilization, should mean the power of taking the animal-man out of his sense-life. (IV. 284)

Civilization is the manifestation of that divinity in man. (V. 308)

## Command

The command will come by itself. (III. 134)

## Compound

No compound can be permanent. (VI. 44)

## Concentration

The power of concentration is the only key to the treasure-house of knowledge. (II. 391)

Concentration is the essence of all knowledge. (VI. 123)

Along with the development of concentration we must develop the power of detachment. (VI. 38)

## Condemnation

Condemnation accomplishes nothing. (VII. 28)

All condemnation of others really condemns ourselves. (VII. 28)

## Consciousness

Consciousness is not co-existent with existence. (IV. 195)

## Contemplation

Continual attention to one object is contemplation. (VII. 68)

## Cowards

Cowards never win victories. (I. 339)

We are all born cowards. (III. 529)

Bullies are always cowards. (VI. 305)

The coward is an object to be pitied. (VIII. 481)

There is no greater sin than cowardice; cowards are never saved—that is sure. (VIII. 481)

Cowardice is no virtue. (V. 86)

## Creation

Inequality is the very basis of creation. (I. 114)

Creation means the struggle to get back to freedom. (I. 422)

Creation came out of the Word. (I. 74)

Creation means a combination which means a certain future dissolution. (I. 8)

Every item of creation is simply a composition. (II. 268)

Creation cannot have either a beginning or an end; it is an eternal on-going. (II. 436)

All this creation, manifestation, cannot be produced out of zero. (II. 425)

In this creation of the impartial Lord, He has made equal every particle in the universe. (III. 158)

Unity is before creation, diversity is creation. (IV. 372)

Variation (*Vichitrata*), that is to say *Jati*, means creation. (IV. 372)

Individuality in universality is the plan of creation. (VI. 121)

Creation is Infinite. (VI. 55)

Creation is infinite, without beginning and without end —the ever-moving ripple in an infinite lake. (VII. 12)

Creation is not a 'making' of something, it is the struggle to regain equilibrium. (VIII. 29)

## Culture

It is culture that withstands shocks, not a simple mass of knowledge. (III. 291)

There must come culture into the blood. (III. 291)

It is spiritual culture and ethical culture alone that can change wrong racial tendencies for the better. (III. 182)

The finer the organism, the higher the culture. (V. 429)

## Death

Death is but a change. (II. 501)

The human soul is eternal and immortal, perfect and infinite, and death means only a change of centre from one body to another. (I. 10)

Death means only a change of garments. (I. 461)

Death is but a change of condition. (IV. 189)

If death comes—that is the worst of our miseries—let it come ! (I. 480)

'Death is better than a vegetating ignorant life; it is better to die on the battle-field than to live a life of defeat.' (II. 124)

Death is the result of inaction. (IV. 127)

Death is the goal of all objects, change is the nature of all objective things. (V. 429)

Death lies in the senses. (V. 267)

Sameness is the sign of death. (VI. 65)

## Democracy

More bread, more opportunity for everybody. (IV. 368)

The new order of things is the salvation of the people by the people. (V. 215-16)

Our masses are gods as compared with those of other countries. (V. 223)

The one problem you have is to give to the masses their rights. (V. 223)

Kings having gone, the power is the people's. (V. 215)

It is the duty of every aristocracy to dig its own grave; and the sooner it does so, the better for all. (V. 214)

## Denunciation

Denunciation is never the highest. (VII. 27)

Denunciation is not at all the way to do good. (III. 195)

## Desire

Desire is without beginning. (I. 296)

There is no limit to man's desires; he goes on desiring, and when he comes to a point where desire cannot be fulfilled, the result is pain. (I. 243)

Desire is infinite, its fulfilment limited. (V. 428)

Desire will not come unless there is something outside to fulfil it. (V. 250)

No desire for the world ! (VI. 90)

The satisfaction of desire only increases it, as oil poured on fire but makes it burn more fiercely (VIII. 22)

Desire is increased by desire. (VIII. 117)

Man's thirst, says the Hindu, man's thirst, says Buddhist, is a burning unquenchable thirst for more and more. (VIII. 250)

Whatever man desires, he gets. (I. 498)

While we hope for anything, desire still rules us (VIII. 22)

There is only one real desire : to know what is true, to be spiritual. (VIII. 118)

Our desires also are constantly changing—what we would prize today we would reject tomorrow. (V. 428)

All desires are but beads of glass. (VII. 10)

All desire is contained in the Self. (II. 468)

It is our desire that binds us. (I. 443)

Desire makes slaves of us. (VIII. 7)

Desire, want, is the father of all misery. (II. 4)

Desires bring all misery. (II. 172)

Desires are bound by the laws of success and failure. (II. 4)

It is the 'desireless' who bring great results to pass. (VIII. 31)

## Destiny

One's destiny is in one's own hands—the Guru only makes this much understood. (VI. 456)

## Detachment

Almost all our suffering is caused by not having the power of detachment. (VI. 38)

There come moments in our life, when we feel our play is finished, and we want to rush to the Mother (Divine). (V. 254)

The fruit falls from the tree when it gets ripe. (V. 45)

No selfishness, no name, no fame, yours or mine, nor my Master's even ! (V. 34)

Unto him comes everything who does not care for anything. (V. 251)

## Difference

Difference makes all beautiful here. (IV. 127)

Difference is the sauce of life, it is the beauty, it is the art of everything. (IV. 127)

Differentiation, infinitely contradictory, must remain, but it is not necessary that we should hate each other therefore; it is not necessary therefore that we should fight each other. (III. 115)

Differentiation is in manifestation. (VI. 34)

## Dirt

Dirt cannot wash dirt; hate cannot cure hate. (II. 495)

... to be a disciple: great preparations
... ...ary; many conditions have to be fulfilled. (III. 107)

**Di...**

A sap... ... must be hedged about for protection, but
when it becomes a tree, a hedge would be a
hindrance. (VIII. 220)

**Discrimination**

Our business is to verify, not to swallow. (VI. 133)

**Divine**

The Divine will look after all. (III. 246)

The Divine within; every being, however degraded, is
the expression of the Divine. (V. 191)

Divinity is our nature. (II. 193)

Consciously or unconsciously, every man is trying to
unfold that divinity. (I. 389)

**Dogmas**

No dogmas will satisfy the cravings of hunger. (III. 432)

**Duty**

No duty is ugly, no duty is impure. (I. 70)

Each duty has its own place, and according to the
circumstances in which we are placed, we must
perform our duties. (I. 47)

Duty for duty's sake; work for work's sake. (I. 442)

Duty is seldom sweet. (I. 67)

Duty is sweet only through love, and love shines in
freedom alone. (I. 67)

Only true duty is to be unattached and to work as free
beings, to give up all work unto God. (I. 103)

Before reaching the highest ideal, man's duty is to evil; let him work, let him fight, let him strike straight from the shoulder. (I. 39)

Our duty is to encourage everyone in his struggle to live up to his own highest ideal, and strive at the same time to make the ideal as near as possible to the truth. (I. 41)

What is duty for one is not duty for another. (I. 47)

All our duties are His. (I. 103)

Ours are the duties. Let the fruits take care of them-selves. (IV. 159)

Every duty is holy, and devotion to duty is the highest form of the worship of God; it is certainly a source of great help in enlightening and emancipating the deluded and ignorance—encumbered souls of the *Baddhas*—the bound ones. (V. 240)

## Education

Education is not filling the mind with a lot of facts. (I. 510)

Education has yet to be in the world, and civilization—civilization has begun nowhere yet. (III. 114)

Education is not the amount of information that is put into your brain and runs riot there, undigested, all your life. (III. 302)

The first duty is to educate the people. (III. 216)

It is man-making education all round that we want. (III. 224)

Education is the manifestation of the perfection already in man. (IV. 358)

Education, education, education alone ! (IV. 483)

We want that education by which character is formed,

strength of mind is increased, the intellect is expanded, and by which one can stand on one's own feet. (V. 342)

To me the very essence of education is concentration of mind, not the collecting of facts. (VI. 38)

Educate your women first and leave them to themselves; then they will tell you what reforms are necessary for them. (VI. 115)

Real education is that which enables one to stand on one's own legs. (VII. 147-48)

If the poor cannot come to education, education must reach them at the plough, in the factory, everywhere. (VIII. 308)

If the poor boy cannot come to education, education must go to him. (IV. 363)

There is only one purpose in the whole of life—education. (VIII. 431)

## Effect

The effect is always the cause worked out. (VI. 125)

## Ego

Truth will never come into our minds so long as there will remain the faintest shadow of *Ahamkara* (egotism). (V. 258)

This rascal ego must be obliterated. (VII. 15)

## Emotions

Emotions many times drag us down to the level of animals. (VI. 7-8)

## End

Let us perfect the means; the end will take care of itself. (II. 9)

## Energies

The sum total of the energies in the universe is the same throughout. (I. 152)

One particle of matter has all the energy of the universe at its back. (VIII. 223)

## Enjoyment

Enjoyment should not be the goal. (I. 88)

Search for enjoyment is vain. (I. 211)

Enjoyment lies not in physical development, but in the culture of the mind and the intellect. (V. 534)

The enjoyment that you are seeking is only in peace; and peace, in the renunciation of physical pleasure. (V. 534)

## Equality

True equality has never been and never can be on earth. (I. 113)

No privilege for anyone, equal chances for all; let every one be taught that the divine is within, and every one will work out his own salvation. (III. 246)

## Error

Error must accompany reason, but the very struggle to conquer error makes us gods. (VIII. 18)

## Essentials

The essentials are eternal, the non-essentials have value only for a certain time and if after a time they are not replaced by something essential, they are positively dangerous. (III. 174-75)

Chastity is the first virtue in man or woman. (I. 67)

Honesty is the best policy, and a virtuous man must gain in the end. (VI. 282)

Perfect sincerity, holiness, gigantic intellect, and an all-conquering will. (VIII. 335)

Obedience is the first duty. (VII. 494)

The only way of getting our divine nature manifested is by helping others to do the same. (VI. 319)

This is the way to perfection, to strive to be perfect, and to strive to make perfect a few men and women. (VIII. 302)

Out of purity and silence comes the word of power. (VIII. 32)

Three things are necessary to make every man great, every nation great :

1. Conviction of the powers of goodness.
2. Absence of jealousy and suspicion.
3. Helping all who are trying to be and do good. (VIII. 299)

One has to be free, and as broad as sky. One has to have a mind that is crystal clear; only then can truth shine in it. (VIII. 104)

Everyone must work out his own salvation. (VIII. 307)

The truth is that so long as the principle, the ideal, of which the outer man is the expression, is not hurt or destroyed, the man lives and there is hope for that man. (VIII. 73)

This I have seen in life—he who is over cautious about himself falls into dangers at every step; he who is afraid of losing honour and respect, gets only disgrace; he who is always afraid of loss always loses. (VIII. 433)

Only that is ours which we earn. (VIII. 15)

Duty of any kind is not to be slighted. (V. 239)

The great secret is—absence of jealousy. (V. 37)

He who wants, gets. (IV. 24)

Our watchword, then, will be acceptance, and not exclusion. (II. 373-74)

That, without which we cannot live, must come to us. (V. 251)

The great lesson to learn is that I am not the standard by which the whole universe is to be judged; each man is to be judged by his own idea, each race by its own standard and ideal, each custom of each country by its own reasoning and conditions. (V. 241)

For our own motherland a junction of the two great systems, Hinduism and Islam—Vedanta brain and Islam body—is the only hope. (VI. 416)

No religion for you, my children, but morality and bravery. (V. 3)

We need to have three things; the heart to feel, the brain to conceive, the hand to work. (VI. 144)

We need a heart to feel, a brain to conceive, and a strong arm to do the work. (VIII. 223)

Sweet words are heard afar, it is particularly necessary to try and make new people come. (VIII. 401)

The only way is love and sympathy. (VIII. 331)

The seed (*Mantra*) must be a living seed, and the field (student) must be ready ploughed; and when both these conditions are fulfilled, a wonderful growth of genuine religion takes place. (III. 46)

We must have life-building, man-making, character-making assimilation of ideas. (III. 302)

We have to take care of what we eat and drink, and what we do. (I. 139)

First bread and then religion. (III. 432)

Worldliness and realization of God cannot go together. (V. 81)

Idleness won't do. (VI. 278)

The world requires a few hundred bold men and women. (II. 85)

We indeed require bold men in this world to tell us bold words about truth. (IV. 277)

A handful of strong men knowing that Self and living in Its light would revolutionize the world. (V. 187)

'This Atman is not to be attained by one who is weak.' (VI. 311)

Bold words and bolder deeds are what we want. (VII. 501)

What we want now is an immense awakening of *Rajasika* energy, for the whole country is wrapped in the shroud of *Tamas*. (V. 403)

Strength, strength is what the Upanishads speak to me from every page. (III. 237)

Fire and enthusiasm must be in our blood. (III. 318)

No cowardice, no sin, no crime, no weakness—the rest will come of itself. (V. 3)

It is gentleness that has the strength to live on and to fructify and not mere brutality and physical force. (III. 188)

By declaring we are weak, we become weak, we do not become better. (VIII. 131)

We want infinite energy, infinite zeal, infinite courage, and infinite patience, then only will great things be achieved. (VI. 384)

Infinite faith and strength are the only conditions of success. (V. 78)

So long as you have faith and honesty and devotion, everything will prosper. (V. 98)

We want *Shraddha*, we want faith in our own selves. (V. 332)

Everything will come to you if you have faith. (V. 62)

We must have plodding industry and perseverance. (VI. 321)

Infinite patience, infinite purity, and infinite perseverance are the secret of success in a good cause. (V. 84)

Great results are attained only by great patience, great courage, and great attempts. (V. 86)

The three great requisites are: Purity

Patience

Perseverance. (VIII. 38)

Patience and steady work—this is the only way. (V. 96)

We must work, and this cannot be done by merely sitting idle. (VI. 287-88)

Men should work for work's sake only, and love for love's sake. (III. 156)

Work, worship, and knowledge are the three steps. (III. 521)

Work, worship, and *Jnana* (Knowledge)—first work, and your mind will be purified; otherwise everything will be fruitless like pouring oblations on a pile of ashes instead of in the sacred fire. (VI. 288)

The first thing necessary is a quiet and peaceable life. (II. 36)

**Eternity**

Everything exists through eternity, and will exist through eternity. (II. 208)

The passage of time makes no mark whatever on the dial of eternity. (IV. 188)

They (Principles of religion) are all built upon the eternal principles that are in man and nature; they can never change. (III. 121)

Every soul moves, as it were, in a circle, and will have to complete it, and no soul can go so low but there will come a time when it will have to go upwards. No one will be lost. (I. 416)

It is true that every being will become free, sooner or later; no one can be lost. (II. 259)

Nothing is lost. (II. 36)

Nothing can come to destruction; everything must come up. (II. 259)

There is nothing new; there will be nothing new. (II. 229)

None was ever born; none will ever die; one changes one's position—that is all. (II. 31)

Really speaking nobody is ever born or dies. (III. 22)

Wealth goes, beauty vanishes, life flies, powers fly— but the Lord abideth for ever, love abideth for ever. (VI. 262)

Real permanence is in Him. (VIII. 213)

That which is self-luminous cannot decay. (II. 215)

The unchangeable alone can be free and, therefore, immortal. (IV. 256)

**Ethics**

Ethics is unity; its basis is love. (I. 432)

**Evil**

Every reaction in the form of hatred or evil is so much loss to the mind; and every evil thought or deed of hatred or any thought of reaction, if it is controlled, will be laid in our favour. (I. 222)

Evil exists, and there is no shirking the fact. (VI. 147)

Each is responsible for the evil anywhere in the world. (VI. 83)

There is nothing that is absolutely evil. (V. 253)

Darkness is less light; evil is less good; impurity is less purity. (II. 327)

When God and good and everything else is in us, there is no evil. (VI. 379)

The 'I' is evil. (VI. 148)

The cause of evil is our desire to be superior to others and our selfishness. (II. 496)

Force against force never cures, and the only cure for evil is unselfishness. (II. 496)

This 'me and mine' is the very root of all the evil in the world. (II. 244)

The evils that are in the world are caused by none else but ourselves. (II. 242)

All evil comes, as our scriptures say, relying upon differences. (III. 194)

I can not see evil unless I be evil. (I. 426)

In doing evil we injure ourselves and others also. (I. 82)

Marriage and sex and money are the only living devils. (V. 138)

## Evolution

Evolution is in nature, not in the soul—evolution of nature, manifestation of the soul. (VI. 92)

The worm of today is the God of tomorrow. (VIII. 250)

Every being that is in the universe has the potentiality of

transcending the senses; even the little worm will one day transcend the senses and reach God. (I. 416)

Every evolution pre-supposes an involution. (II. 75)

Every evolution is preceded by an involution. (V. 255)

Evolution does not come out of zero. (II. 228)

Every evolution here is the evolution of something which existed previously. (V. 255)

The true secret of evolution is the manifestation of the perfection which is already in every being. (I. 292)

Nothing can be evolved which is not already there. (II. 227)

Instinct develops into reason, and reason into the transcendental consciousness. (I. 185)

We are all born savages and gradually civilize ourselves. (I. 490)

The dry, abstract Advaita must become living—poetic—in everyday life; out of hopelessly intricate mythology must come concrete moral forms; and out of bewildering *Yogism* must come the most scientific and practical psychology—and all this must be put in a form so that a child may grasp it. (V. 104-5)

Before you were an animal, now you are a man, and will be a god or God Himself in future. (VII. 445)

We stand in the present, but open ourselves to the infinite future. (II. 374)

All the heaven that ever existed is now and here. (II. 372)

We must not remain children for ever. (I. 325)

Every fool may become a hero at one time or another. (I. 29)

## Experience

Experience is the only source of knowledge. (VIII. 428)

Experience is the one teacher, the one eye-opener. (VIII. 492-93)

## Expression

Many feel, but only a few can express. (VIII. 428)

Without expression, how can we live ? (III. 441)

## Existence

The real existence is without manifestation. (V. 274)

## Failure

There is no such thing as failure in the universe. (I. 416)

There is success and failure in every work. (VIII. 430)

## Faith

Faith is not belief, it is the grasp on the Ultimate, an illumination. (VII. 60)

He who has no faith in himself can never have faith in God. (I. 38)

A man must not only have faith but intellectual faith too. (V. 244)

Faith is one of the potent factors of humanity and of all religions. (III. 444)

Faith, faith, faith in ourselves, faith, faith in God—this is the secret of greatness. (III. 190)

It is faith that makes a lion of a man. (V. 99)

The essence of our Faith consists simply in this freedom of the *Ishta*. (V. 235)

So long as you have faith in your guru, nothing will be able to obstruct your way. (V. 106)

This *Shraddha* must enter into you. (III. 319)

## Fame

Fame does not pay, nor learning. (IV. 367)

The most insidious is the love of fame. (V. 413)

## Fanatics

Fanatics are indeed the sincerest of mankind. (I. 113)

The fanatic loses all power of judgement. (III. 33)

Fanatics only make hatred. (V. 244)

This disease of fanaticism is one of the most dangerous
of all diseases. (II. 377)

## Fate

Each one of us is the maker of his own fate. (III. 125)

## Fault

Never forget that a man is made great and perfect as
much by his faults as by his virtues. (VIII. 269)

We do not look at our own faults; the eyes do not see
themselves, they see the eyes of everybody
else. (II. 224)

## Fear

And because that nature is selfless, it is strong and
fearless; for only to selfishness comes fear. (II. 357)

Fear is a sign of weakness. (I. 47)

Fear is the mother of all (misery). (I. 480)

Fear ceases, and then alone come perfect happiness and
perfect love. (II. 415)

The greatest sin is fear. (V. 35)

Fear is death—fear is the greatest sin. (VII. 200)

Fear is death, fear is sin, fear is hell, fear is
unrighteousness, fear is wrong life. (VII. 136)

It is fear alone that is death. (VI. 473)

Fear is the cause of degradation and sin. (III. 160)

It is fear that brings misery, fear that brings death, fear
that breeds evil. (III. 160)

It is fear that is the great cause of misery in the
    world. (III. 321)

It is fear that is the greatest of all superstitions. (III. 321)

It is fear that is the cause of our woes, and it is fearlessness
    that brings heaven even in a moment. (III. 321)

Fear is one of our worst enemies. (VIII. 4)

The moment you fear, you are nobody. (III. 321)

Those who are protected by the Lord must be above fear.
    (VI. 342)

## Fearless

You are fearless and deathless only when you are the
    universe. (III. 417)

## Fearlessness

The only religion that ought to be taught is the religion
    of *fearlessness*. (III. 160)

## Feeling

It is feeling that is the life, the strength, the vitality,
    without which no amount of intellectual activity can
    reach God. (II. 307)

It is through the feelings that the highest secrets are
    reached. (III. 318)

Feeling is the soul, the secret of everything. (VII. 407)

## Finite

We can have no idea of a thing unless it is finite. (VI. 108)

## Food

Certain regulations as to food are necessary; we must
    use that food which brings us the purest mind.
    (I. 136)

Pure food brings a pure mind and in a pure mind is a
    constant memory of God. (IV. 6)

Pure food, no doubt, helps pure thought; it has an intimate connection; both ought to be there. (III. 339)

All exciting food should be avoided. (IV. 4)

## Force

Force cannot exist without matter. (I. 395)

No force can die, no matter can be annihilated. (II. 231)

Every force completes a circuit. (VI. 138)

## Form

Whatever is form must break some time or other. (I. 494)

Everything that occupies space has form. (VI. 21)

The forms have value only so far as they are expressions of the life within. (III. 68)

The forms are evanescent; but the spirit, being in the Lord and of the Lord, is immortal and omnipresent. (VII. 500)

All forms are transitory, that is why all religions say 'God has no form'. (VIII. 16)

Everything that has form must have a beginning and an end. (II. 254)

Everything which has names and forms is transient. (II. 315-16)

Everything that has name and form must begin in time, exist in time, and end in time. (II. 316)

Everything which has name and form must die. (II. 316)

## Free

Only the free have free will. (VII. 99)

Duty ceases for him who is free. (VIII. 26)

He who asserts he is free, shall be free. (VI. 311)

To be free one must be above the laws of nature. (VI. 84)

What you do not make free, will never grow. (II. 115)

The solution of the Vedanta is that we are not bound, we are free already. (II. 197-98)

If you dare declare that you are free, free you are this moment. (II. 350)

The unchangeable alone can be free and, therefore, immortal. (IV. 256)

We must always bear in mind that we are not going to be free, but are free already. (III. 16)

We, we, and none else, are responsible for what we suffer. (III. 125)

There is something in us which is free and permanent. (IV. 255-56)

We have got to work and worship and struggle to be free. (III. 16)

No man is free who is subject to the bondage of matter. (III. 139)

He (free man) does good, because it is his nature, not because any fancied duty commands it. (VIII. 26)

It is man's ceaseless endeavour to become free. (I. 335)

We want to know in order to make ourselves free. (IV. 240)

If we are not free, how can we hope to make the world better? (IV. 190)

The free must certainly be beyond cause and effect. (I. 254)

A man should be free to think, especially spiritual thoughts. (VIII. 302)

To have nobody to care for and never minding who cares for one is the way to be free. (VIII. 414)

A perfect, free being cannot have any desire. (II. 261)

## Freedom

The goal of the soul is freedom. (III. 127)

'Freedom, O Freedom ! Freedom, O Freedom !' is the song of the soul. (I. 335)

Freedom is its (self's) nature, its birthright. (II. 323)

Freedom is its (self's) watchword. (II. 323)

Everywhere we see this assertion of freedom, this freedom of the soul. (II. 400)

Freedom is of the nature of the soul, it is its birthright. (II. 282)

The search for freedom is the search of all religions. (II. 400)

This freedom is the goal towards which we are all moving. (II. 256)

Freedom is the motive of the universe, freedom its goal. (V. 434)

Freedom is the goal. (V. 289)

What is the goal? It is freedom. (VI. 57)

Freedom is the one goal of all nature, sentient or insentient; and consciously or unconsciously, everything is struggling towards that goal. (I. 109)

All nature is crying through all the atoms for one thing—its perfect freedom. (IV. 241)

*Freedom* is the goal of the Universe. (VIII. 344)

Every one is struggling for freedom—from the atom to the star. (V. 288)

Let us then be brave and sincere : whatever path we follow with devotion, must take us to freedom. (VIII. 27)

Within ourselves is this eternal voice speaking of eternal freedom; its music is eternally going on. (II. 325)

Freedom is the test of the higher being. (VIII. 40)

To become pure is the shortest path to freedom. (VIII. 15)

Freedom is never to be reached by the weak. (I. 146)

No freedom without renunciation. (VI. 505)

We seek neither misery nor happiness, but freedom. (VIII. 250)

What we want is freedom, not life, nor pleasure, nor good. (VIII. 30; VII. 12)

Only freedom can produce true morality. (VIII. 27)

Freedom means immortality. (VI. 84)

Nature with its infinite power is only a machine; freedom alone constitutes sentient life. (V. 289)

Freedom already *is*. (V. 317)

Man has freedom already, but he will have to discover it. (V. 288)

To advance oneself towards freedom—physical, mental, and spiritual—and help others to do so, is the supreme prize of man. (V. 147)

The word freedom which is the watchword of our religion really means freedom physically, mentally, and spiritually. (V. 216)

Freedom in all matters, i.e. advance towards *Mukti* is the worthiest gain of man. (V. 147)

We say that it is freedom that we are to seek, and that that freedom is God. (V. 288)

There is no other purpose in life, save to reach this freedom. (I. 340)

The goal of all nature is freedom, and freedom is to be attained only by perfect unselfishness. (I. 110)

Freedom is not here, but is only to be found beyond. (I. 99)

Freedom breathes in the throb of the universe. (I. 338)

Freedom is inseparably connected with immortality. (VI. 84)

We never get freedom until we are self-contained. (VII. 91)

Freedom is to lose all illusions. (VII. 34)

In and through all the literature voicing man's struggle towards freedom, towards universal freedom, again and again you find the Indian Vedantic ideals coming out prominently. (III. 189)

Wherever there is life, there is this search for freedom and that freedom is the same as God. (I. 337)

We are here for freedom, for knowledge. (IV. 239)

The greatest goodness is the highest freedom. (VI. 100)

Freedom means independence of anything outside, and that means that nothing outside itself could work upon it as a cause (II. 196)

There is no freedom until you go beyond Maya. (III. 14)

There is no freedom in Maya. (III. 14)

Not one atom can rest until it finds its freedom. (VII. 99)

The highest state is when we have no desires, but the two are opposite poles of the same existence. (II. 261-62)

Every man has to make his own choice; so has every nation. (III. 221)

Whether we know it or not, whether we are conscious or unconscious of it, we are all working to get out of the dream of the world. (I. 99)

We must inform our minds that no one in this universe depends upon us. (I. 89)

No one was ever bound. (I. 500)

Everything in the universe is struggling for liberty. (VIII. 249)

Liberty is the only condition of growth. (IV. 346)

Liberty is the first condition of growth. (III. 246)

There cannot be any growth without liberty. (IV. 367)

Denial of the will to live, knowledge, and same-
sightedness is the trinity of liberation. (VIII. 344)
Liberation consists in knowing our unity with the
wonderful Impersonality. (III. 129)

### Futile

Criticism and destruction are of no avail. (VI. 142)
Idle gossip and barren ceremonials won't do. (VI. 293)

### Future

Out of the past is built the future. (III. 285-86)

### Gerua

The *Gerua* robe is not for enjoyment. It is the banner of
heroic work. (VI. 288)

### Gift

The highest of gifts is the giving of spiritual knowledge.
(III. 133)
Giving alone is the one work in this *Kali Yuga*; of all the
gifts, giving spiritual life is the highest gifts possible.
(III. 167-68)

### Gita

The *Gita* is like a bouquet composed of the beautiful
flowers of spiritual truths collected from the
Upanishads. (II. 189)
Than the *Gita* no better commentary on the Vedas has
been written or can be written. (III. 261)
Work, work, work, day and night, says the *Gita*. (IV. 130)
This knowledge of Atman is the highest aim of the
*Gita*. (VII. 199)
This is the central idea of the *Gita*—to be calm and

steadfast in all circumstances, with one's body, mind, and soul centred at His hallowed feet ! (VII. 273)

## Goal

The goal of the universe is to realize oneness with the 'Om' or One Existence. (VIII. 11)

Pure Existence-Knowledge-and-Love is the goal. (VI.133)

Wisdom (*Jnana*) is the goal of all life. (III. 4)

The goal of mankind is knowledge. (I. 27)

This is the goal of the Vedantin, to attain freedom while living. (II. 281)

The goal of man is to go beyond law. (I. 451)

Our goal is freedom, our goal is unselfishness. (I. 115)

The goal of all nature is freedom. (I. 110)

That is the goal, the infinite realm of the super-conscious. (II. 35)

Absolute control of nature, and nothing short of it, must be the goal. (I. 140)

The goal is to manifest this Divinity within, by controlling nature, external and internal. (I. 257)

The goal of man is neither misery nor happiness, but we have to be master of that out of which these are manufactured. (I. 452)

To see God is the one goal. (VI. 133)

God is the one goal of all our passions and emotions. (III. 97)

Eternal Bliss is our goal. (III. 128)

The aim, the end, the goal, of all this training is liberation of the soul. (I. 140)

The knowledge of Brahman is the ultimate goal—the highest destiny of man. (VII. 197)

Our goal is to perceive the soul itself. (I. 234)

The goal of each soul is freedom, mastery—freedom from the slavery of matter and thought, mastery of external and internal nature. (I. 172)

The end is the realization of Brahman. (VII. 198)

Realizing my own real nature is the one goal of my life. (V. 253)

Death for the cause is our goal, not success. (VIII. 522)

What we want is progress, development, realization. (II. 336)

The end and aim of all training is to make the man grow. (II. 15)

## Gold

This race after gold and power is all vanity of vanities. (III. 182)

## God

God is love personified. (III. 365)

God is love, and only he who has known God as love can be a teacher of godliness and God to man. (III. 51)

All loves and all passions of the human heart must go to God. (III. 98)

The God of love is the one thing to be worshipped. (III. 365)

He is the Beloved. (III. 98)

He is beauty itself, sublimity itself. (III. 98)

He is in fact the only attraction worthy of human hearts. (III. 75)

We are all women; there are no men in this world; there is but One man, and this is He, our Beloved. (III. 96)

Everywhere is the same God, the All-love. (IV. 496)

His love never fails. (IV. 129)

This love of God cannot be reached by the weak. (IV. 60)

Who loves all beings without distinction, He indeed is worshipping best his God. (IV. 496)

Wherever we are and whatever we do, He is ever and ever the same merciful, the same loving heart. (IV. 129)

We must love Him, and everyone that lives—only in and through Him. (IV. 129)

God is a circle whose circumference is nowhere and whose centre is everywhere. (VIII. 9)

Man is an infinite circle whose circumference is nowhere, but the centre is located in a spot, and God is an infinite circle whose circumference is nowhere, but whose centre is everywhere (II. 33)

God is love, and love is God. (VI. 73)

God is the only love. (V. 417)

Pure Existence-Knowledge-and-Love is the goal; and Love is God. (VI. 133)

Love is God, freedom is God; and everything that is bondage is not God. (V. 288)

The very idea of God is love. (VII. 29)

He is the only object to be loved. (I. 12)

God is only to be loved. (II. 245)

He, as love, is self-evident. (III. 91)

God is all there is. (VI. 53)

God is the eternal life of the universe. (VI. 94)

God is the highest form of generalized law. (VI. 110)

God is Infinite. (III. 513)

God is perfect: He has no wants. (III. 94)

God is the only dispenser of results; leave it to Him to do all that. (VI. 455)

God Himself is your image. (III. 24)

God has created me and I have created God. (VII. 29)

God is the big magician; He does all the tricks. (VI. 74)

God is present in every Jiva; there is no other God besides that. (VII. 247)

God is as man is. (VIII. 256)

God can only be known in and through man. (VIII. 298)

The highest concept we can have of God is man. (VIII. 34)

The highest ideal of every man is called God. (III. 89)

God is life; God is truth. (VIII. 106)

God is *true*, all else is *nothing*. (VIII. 166)

God exists, nothing else exists, everything else comes and goes. (VIII. 107)

God is true, and the world is not true. (VIII. 107)

The only object unchangeable and the only complement of character and aspirations of the human Soul is God. (V. 426)

Unselfishness is God. (I. 87)

God is in everything, where else shall we go to find Him? (II. 150)

God is personal and impersonal at the same time. (II. 323)

God is a person only apparently, but really He is the Impersonal Being. (II. 192)

God is the Soul of all souls and the whole of nature. (II. 192)

They start with the assertion that God is both the efficient and the material cause of the universe. (II. 245)

God is the centre of attraction for every soul. (II. 244)

God is the magnet and human soul is the needle. (II. 244)

A God known is no more God; He has become finite like one of us. (II. 133)

God is not the world. (I. 87)

God is omnipresent, He is manifesting Himself in every being; but for men, He is only visible, recognizable, in man. (II. 42)

God alone is eternal, and everything else is transitory. (I. 411)

God is here, in all these human souls. (I. 424)

God comes to you in the blind, in the halt, in the poor, in the weak, in the diabolical. (I. 442)

God is not to be made, but He already exists. (I. 434)

God is the Teacher of all teachers, because these teachers, however great they may have been—gods or angels—were all bound and limited by time, while God is not. (I. 217)

God is omnipresent. (I. 495)

God is ever present therein, He is undying and—eternally active and infinitely watchful. (I. 80)

God was your own reflection cast upon the screen of Maya. (I. 500)

God is true. (I. 501)

God is unattached because He loves; that real love makes us unattached. (I. 58)

The Impersonal God is a living God, a principle. (II. 319)

If you are not God, there never was any God, and never will be. (II. 308)

Seeing God is the aim and goal of all human life. (I. 319)

The concept of God is a fundamental element in human constitution. (I. 334)

The knowledge of God is the highest knowledge, and knowing God alone we can know man. (I. 433)

We are born of Him, we live in Him, and unto Him we return. (II. 211)

All scriptures preach that we come from God and go back to God. (II. 210)

He is the Essence of all this, the Soul of my soul. (II. 133)

He is the Essence of our own Self. (II. 133)

Only truth is *He* the living ! (VIII. 166)

If there is a God, He is in our own hearts. (II. 163)

All this is not, God alone is ! (V. 72)

God is in every man, whether man knows it or not. (V. 148)

The real happiness is God. (V. 288)

Matter can never be your God; body can never be your God. (IV. 352)

Dualism is the natural idea of the senses; as long as we are bound by the senses we are bound to see a God who is only Personal and nothing but Personal, we are bound to see the world as it is. (III. 349)

The Personal God is therefore the highest conception of human nature. (III. 257)

The Personal God worshipped by the *Bhakta* is not separate or different from the Brahman. (III. 37)

The Personal God is the Absolute looked at through the haze of Maya—ignorance. (VIII. 255)

The life of God is infinite. (I. 107)

I see God, therefore He exists. (I. 483)

A changeable God would be no God. (I. 418)

There is One who never changes, and that is God. (I. 412)

The one thing unchangeable is God. (VI. 109)

As long as we are men, we must worship Him in man and as man. (III. 54)

No man can really see God except through these human manifestations. (III. 53)

Losing faith in one's self means losing faith in God. (III. 376)

The first gods we have to worship are our country-men. (III. 301)

The nearer we approach God, the more do we begin to see that all things are in Him. (III. 82)

Everything in this world, whether good or bad, belongs to God. (III. 365)

God and soul are the only realities, infinitely more real than the world. (IV. 305)

We cannot understand God in our scriptures without knowing the soul. (III. 125)

You are God. (IV. 237)

To know God is to become God. (IV. 342)

There is not one system in India which does not hold the doctrine that God is within, that Divinity resides within all things. (III. 191)

He is in the heart of our hearts. (II. 401)

He is always in us and with us. (II. 174)

The God in you is the God in all. (I. 429)

He is all. (V. 254)

He is the all in all; He is all and in all. (I. 107)

We all came from God and we are all bound to go back to God. (I. 197)

Here He is in the heart of man, the Soul of our souls, the Reality in us. (I. 356)

God is Spirit, is infinite, man is Spirit and, therefore, infinite, and the Infinite alone can worship the Infinite. (I. 341)

God is man's very Self. (VIII. 127)

Every being is divine, is God. (IV. 357)

God manifests Himself to you in man. (IV. 151)

Through soul, therefore, the analysis of the human soul alone, can we understand God. (III. 125)

Everywhere is He. (V. 336)

He is in everything, He is everything. (II. 326)

Everything is the living God, the living Christ; see it as such. (VII. 89)

There is only one ruler of the universe, and that is God. (I. 398)

He is everywhere, the pure and formless One, the Almighty and the All-merciful. (I. 11)

He is the Oneness, the Unity of all, the Reality of all life and all existence. (II. 306)

The sum total of the whole universe is God Himself. (I. 375)

The whole universe is a symbol, and God is the essence behind. (I. 72)

The external aspect of the thought of God is the Word, and as God thought and willed before He created, creation came out of the Word. (I. 74)

In this world nothing is permanent except God. (I. 512)

He is the reality in everything. (III. 422)

It is He Himself who has become this universe. (III. 7)

All roads lead to God. (VIII. 254)

Let each man see and take of God whatever is suitable to Him. (VI. 120)

Without renunciation God can never be realized. (V. 397)

Purity of heart will bring the vision of God. (VII. 103)

Theorising about God will not do; we must love and work. (VII. 9)

The way to God is the opposite to that of the world.
(VII. 467)

The name of God is greater than God. (VIII. 270)

Repeating the name of God has wonderful power.
(VI. 90)

The name of God is everything. (VIII. 270)

Wherever His name is spoken, that place is holy. (IV. 28)

God comes to those who work hard. (VIII. 101)

He never leaves His servant. (VIII. 316)

God alone can worship God. (VIII. 190)

It is God who works, not you. (VIII. 223)

Hatred is a thing which greatly impedes the course of *Bhakti*; and the man who hates none reaches God. (III. 358)

God is not to be reached by the weak. (IV. 11)

God does not reason. (V. 273)

God has become man; man will become God again. (V. 410)

All the Gods are here. (II. 325)

Every religion is only evolving a God out of the material man, and the same God is the inspirer of all of them (religions). (I. 18)

The Absolute Truth is God alone. (VII. 120)

God is life; God is Truth. (VIII. 106)

What we see is God percolating through nature. (VII. 6)

God and freedom are One and the same. (VIII. 236)

This life is not real. The real is God. (VIII. 74)

We can have no conception of God higher than man, so our God is man, and man is God. (VII. 30)

It is impossible to find God outside of ourselves. (VII. 59)

God alone is our goal. Failing to reach God, we die. (VIII. 37)

God is the ideal through which man may see all. (VIII. 222)

As I am the soul of nature, so is God, the soul of my soul. (VIII. 191)

Without seeing the Son, you *cannot* see the Father. (VIII. 190)

God is the infinite, impersonal being—ever existent, unchanging, immortal, fearless; and you are all His incarnations, His embodiments. (VIII. 134)

Blessed is the man who is mad after God. (IV. 172)

He who desires God will get Love, unto him God gives Himself. (IV. 20)

When the heart has been purified, into that heart will come the love of God. (II. 244)

If the mother is pleased, and the father, God is pleased with the man. (I. 43)

All are manifestations of the same Lord. (II. 396)

In life and in death, in happiness and in misery, the Lord is equally present. (II. 146)

We have to cover everything with the Lord Himself. (II. 146)

The Lord can never be hoodwinked. (VIII. 88)

To Him who has nothing in the universe, the Lord comes. (VII. 10)

The Lord will guide, in His own time. (VIII. 336)

In this body He resides, the Lord of all souls and King of kings. (VIII. 135)

While there is a body and we see it, we have not realized God. (VII. 104)

We throw a net and catch something, and then say that

we have demonstrated it; but never, never can we catch God in a net. (VII. 10)

We want everything but God, because our ordinary desires are fulfilled by the external world. (VII. 83)

So long as our needs are confined within the limits of the physical universe, we do not feel any need for God; it is only when we have had hard blows in our lives and are disappointed with everything here that we feel the need for something higher; then we seek God. (VII. 83)

With God every knowledge is sacred. (VIII. 137)

In worshipping God we have been always worshipping our own hidden Self. (II. 279)

Whether we will it or not, we shall have to return to our origin which is called God or Absolute. (I. 197)

It is not at all necessary to be educated or learned to get to God. (I. 413)

The embodiment of freedom, the Master of nature, is what we call God. (I. 336)

No book, ever created God, but God inspired all the great books. (I. 324)

This universal intelligence is what we call God. (II. 210)

He reveals Himself to the pure heart. (I. 13)

If no God, what is the use of life? (II. 473)

It is He who is in the child, in the wife, and in the husband; it is He who is in the good and in the bad; He is in the sin and in the sinner; He is in life and in death. (II. 147)

He is neither evil, nor good; He is the best. (II. 420)

He is not a God outside, but He is inside. (I. 356)

He is working incessantly; all the changes and manifestations of the world are His. (I. 80)

There is no sweetness but He. (II. 421)

He is all contradictions. (VI. 117)

He knows where the bark will reach the shore. (VI. 287)

He makes the dumb fluent. (VI. 287)

He who makes the dumb eloquent and the lame cross a mountain, He will help me. (VIII. 328)

He exists; nothing else does. (VIII. 345)

He is principle, not person. (VIII. 133)

He plays in every atom; He is playing when He is building up earths, and suns, and moons; He is playing with the human heart, the animals, with plants. (III. 95)

He the boundless, the ever-merciful, is always ready to help us to the other shore, for His mercy is great, and it always comes to the pure in Heart. (III. 161)

Deny everything that is not God. (VIII. 228)

God, though everywhere, we can only conceive Him as a big man. (VIII. 298)

Man will ever personify his God in order to worship Him. (VIII. 33)

There is only one thing that is real—God. (VIII. 120)

God helps them that help themselves. (VIII. 101)

To know God, no philosophy is necessary. (VIII. 230)

You are all Gods, says the Vedanta. (VIII. 125)

All knowledge is in God. (III. 514)

God is eternally creating—is never at rest. (III. 122)

There is but one attractive power and, that is God. (III. 365)

Ignorant or wise, saint or sinner, man or woman, educated or uneducated, cultivated or uncultivated, to every human being the highest ideal is God. (III. 89)

The idea of God was nowhere else ever so fully developed as in this motherland of ours, for the same idea of God never existed anywhere else. (III. 154)

Everything must go down before the will, for that comes from God and God Himself; a pure and a strong will is omnipotent. (III. 224)

The highest direction is that which takes us to God; every other direction is lower. (III. 78)

'God has no Form'. (VIII. 16)

We may worship a picture as God, but not God as the picture. (IV. 47)

God in the picture is right, but the picture as god is wrong. (IV. 47)

The memory of God will not come to the selfish man. (IV. 9)

Darkness and light, enjoyment of the world and enjoyment of God will never go together. (IV. 180)

Where the world is, there is no God. (IV. 244)

So long as there is selfishness, in the heart, so long is love of God impossible. (III. 258)

Where God is, there is no other. (IV. 244)

Each one sees God according to his own nature; and this vision, conditioned by our own nature, is our *Ishta*. (IV. 53)

Ishvara is the highest manifestation of the Absolute Reality, or in other words, the higher possible reading of the Absolute by the human mind. (III. 37)

He never changes, He is never angry, whatever we do. (IV. 129)

He has patience, infinite patience. (IV. 129)

We want everything but God. (II. 45)

Who wants God ? That is the question. (II. 44)

When God vanishes, then also vanish the body and mind; and when both vanish, that which is the Real Existence remains for ever. (III. 15)

God never worships God. (IV. 31)

God cannot be worshipped; He is immanent Being of the Universe. (IV. 31)

He who has known God has become God. (IV. 226)

## Good

Contact with holy men is good. (VI. 118)

There is no good, and there is no evil. (VI. 53)

There are good and evil everywhere in the world. (VI. 54)

It is only by doing good to others that one attains to one's own good, and it is by leading others to *Bhakti* and *Mukti* that one attains them oneself. (VI. 266)

I can secure my own good only by doing you good. (VI. 317)

It is preferable to live on grass for the sake of doing good to others. (VI. 288)

Disease and misfortune come to do us good in the long run. (VI. 429)

What is good for you may not be good for others. (VI. 435)

There is no good in store so long as malice and jealousy and egotism will prevail. (VI. 304)

Everything works for the best. (VII. 470)

Doing good is not always smooth ! (VIII. 511)

The road to the Good is the roughest and steepest in the universe. (VIII. 383)

All is good ! (VIII. 505)

The highest good is the realization of the Self. (VIII. 3)

The heart and core of everything here is good, that whatever may be the surface waves, deep down and underlying everything, there is an infinite basis of goodness and love. (VIII. 296)

Goodness is strength. (IV. 133)

Truth is infinitely more weighty than untruth; so is goodness. (V. 65)

More of goodness, less of artificial laws. (VI. 100)

## Grace

There is no condition in grace. (VI. 482)

The wind of His grace is always blowing, what you need to do is to unfurl your sail. (VI. 481)

Those who are pure always in body, mind, and speech, who have strong devotion, who discriminate between the real and the unreal, who persevere in meditation and contemplation—upon them alone the grace of the Lord descends. (VI. 481)

He on whom His grace descends, in a moment goes beyond all law. (VI. 482)

## Great

Each (the *Sannyasi* and the householder) is great in his own place. (I. 47)

## Growth

Growth must proceed from within. (V. 198)

Liberty is the first condition of growth. (VI. 367)

## Guna

A pleasurable feeling is the nature of the *Sattva*. (I. 264)

## Guru/Teacher

The guru is the bright mask which God wears in order to come to us. (VIII. 117)

It is not possible for everyone to be an *Acharya*. (V. 268)

It is the knowledge of the *spirit* of the scriptures alone that constitutes the true religious teacher. (III. 49)

There is no other teacher but your own soul. (V. 410)

Find the teacher, serve him as a child, open your heart to his influence, see in him God manifested. (IV. 28)

Only the knowers of Brahman are the spiritual teachers of mankind. (VI. 464)

The greatness of a teacher consists in the simplicity of his language. (V. 106)

The guru must be a man who has known, has actually realized the Divine truth, has perceived himself as the spirit. (VIII. 115)

One who has known God can alone be a teacher. (IV. 27)

He alone teaches who has something to give. (IV. 177-78)

The guru is the means of realization. (V. 323)

He is an *Acharya* through whom the divine power acts. (V. 268)

It is easier to become a *Jivanmukta* (free in this very life) than to be an *Acharya*. (V. 268)

Anyone and everyone cannot be an *Acharya* (teacher of mankind); but many may become *Mukta* (liberated). (V. 268)

The guru only knows what will lead towards perfection. (V. 258)

Know it for certain that without steady devotion for the guru and unflinching patience and perseverance, nothing is to be achieved. (VII. 447)

*Wah Guru Ki Fateh !* Victory unto the guru !! (VI. 421)

The guru has to bear the disciple's burden of sin. (V. 268)

The power that can transform life in a moment can be found only in the living illuminated souls, those shining lights who appear among us from time to time. (VIII. 116)

The one who has the power of transmitting this current is called a guru. (VI. 141)

The guru is the conveyance in which the spiritual influence is brought to you. (VII. 63)

Nothing, I say, can be done without the chain of discipleship, that is, the power that is transmitted from the guru to the disciple, and from him to his disciple, and so on. (VI. 265)

Without an unbroken chain of discipleship—*Guruparampara*—nothing can be done. (VI. 265)

The real guru is he who leads you beyond this Maya of endless birth and death—who graciously destroys all the griefs and maladies of the soul. (VI. 471)

Nothing can be done without a guru. (VII. 63)

The father and mother give me this body; but the guru gives me rebirth in the soul. (VIII. 112)

The guru frees my soul. (VIII. 112)

A mere talker cannot be the guru. (VIII. 115)

*Gurubhakti* is the foundation of all spiritual development. (V. 98)

Mind you, the *Gurubhakta* will conquer the world—this is the one evidence of history. (V. 99)

**Habit**

The only remedy for bad habits is counter habits. (I. 208)

**Happiness**

He who is alone is happy. (VIII. 414)

If I am unhappy, it has been of my own making, and that everything shows that I can be happy if I will. (III. 125)

There is no happiness higher than what a man obtains by this attitude of non-offensiveness, to all creation. (I. 189)

Happiness belongs to him who knows this oneness, who knows he is one with this universe. (I. 374)

The animal has its happiness in the senses, the man in his intellect, and the God in spiritual contemplation. (I. 186)

Happiness is only found in the Spirit. (II. 83)

Happiness is not in this heaven or in that heaven, it is in the soul. (II.184)

Real happiness is not in the senses but above the senses. (V. 283)

The power of suffering is infinitely greater than the power of doing; the power of love is infinitely of greater potency than the power of hatred. (IV. 348)

## Harmony

God will come to everyone, harmony is within the reach of all. (VII. 24)

We want harmony, not one-sided development. (II. 143)

We want today that bright sun of intellectuality joined with the heart of Buddha, the wonderful infinite heart of love and mercy. (II. 140)

What is now wanted is a combination of the greatest heart with the highest intellectuality, of infinite love with infinite knowledge. (II. 143)

What we really want is head and heart combined. (II. 145)

What we want is the harmony of Existence, Knowledge, and Bliss Infinite. (II. 143)

Too much of everything is bad. (VII. 482)

**Haste**

Nothing shall be done in haste. (VI. 281)

No man ought to take a hasty step. (VI. 80)

**Hatred**

Love is truth, and hatred is false, because hatred makes for multiplicity. (II. 304)

It is hatred that separates man from man, therefore it is wrong and false. (II. 304)

**Health**

We must not forget that health is only a means to an end. (I. 139)

Consciously or unconsciously, health can be trans-mitted. (I. 154)

**Heart**

It is the heart that is of most importance. (II. 306)

Learning and wisdom are superfluities, the surface glitter merely, but it is the heart that is the seat of all power. (VI. 425)

It is always the heart that speaks in the man of love. (I. 413)

Within the heart is the ocean of Love. (IV. 496)

It is through the heart, and the heart alone, that inspiration comes. (III. 318)

Through the heart comes inspiration. (III. 225)

Deep as the ocean, broad as the infinite skies, that is the sort of heart we want. (III. 174)

Heart speaks unto heart better than any language of the mouth. (III. 146)

It is nothing until you have the heart to feel. (III. 432)

It is through the heart that the Lord is seen, and not through the intellect. (II. 306)

Through the heart the Lord speaks, and through the intellect you yourself speak. (I. 415)

When there is conflict between the heart and the brain, let the heart be followed. (I. 412)

It is the heart, the heart that conquers, not the brain. (VI. 400)

It is the heart and the brain that do it ever and ever and not the purse. (VI. 302)

It is the culture of the heart, really, and not that of the intellect that will lessen the misery of the world. (I. 414)

It is the heart which takes one to the highest plane, which intellect can never reach; it goes beyond intellect, and reaches to what is called inspiration. (I. 413)

Always cultivate the heart. (I. 415)

A pure heart sees beyond the intellect. (I. 414)

The pure heart is the best mirror for the reflection of truth, so all these disciplines are for the purification of the heart. (I. 414)

All truth in the universe will manifest in your heart, if you are sufficiently pure. (I. 414)

It is the heart that reaches the Goal. (I. 414)

It is through the *heart*, and that alone, that the world can be reached. (VIII. 406)

'Out of the fullness of the heart the mouth speaketh,' and out of the fullness of the heart the hand works too. (II. 152)

It is culture of the heart that we want. (IV. 222)

He whose book of the heart has been opened needs no
other books. (V. 410)

If one has the colour of the heart, he does not want any
external colour. (III. 283)

The man of heart can never be a devil. (I. 413)

Men of heart get the 'butter', and the 'butter milk' is left
for the intellectual. (I. 413)

Through Hell to Heaven is always the way. (V. 252)

If there is any road to Heaven it is through Hell. (V. 252)

## Help

All search is vain, until we begin to perceive that
knowledge is within ourselves, that no one can help
us, that we must help ourselves. (I. 258)

If we cannot help ourselves, there is none to help us.
(I. 478)

We are our own help. (I. 478)

All the help that has come was from within yourselves. (II. 324)

Help does not come from without; it comes from within
ourselves. (II. 356)

There is no help for you outside of yourself; you are the
creator of the universe. (III. 26)

If you want to help others, your little self must go. (III. 431)

In helping the world we really help ourselves. (I. 80)

Helping others is only helping ourselves. (I. 75)

It is blasphemy to think that you can help anyone. (I. 441-42)

## Hero

Our heroes must be spiritual. (III. 315)

Heroes only enjoy the world. (V. 448)

It is the hero alone, not the coward, who has liberation within his easy reach. (VII. 504)

Defeat is the ornament the hero adorns himself with. (VIII. 432)

## Hilarity

Excessive hilarity is quite as objectionable as too much of sad seriousness. (III. 69)

## Himalayas

The Himalayas stand for that renunciation. (III. 353-54)

## Hindu

The Hindu understands religion and religion alone. (III. 165)

The Hindu man drinks religiously, sleeps religiously, walks religiously, marries religiously, robs religiously. (VIII. 74)

If a Hindu is not spiritual, I do not call him a Hindu. (III. 371)

If any of you do not believe it, if there be a Hindu boy amongst us who is not ready to believe that his religion is pure spirituality, I do not call him a Hindu. (III. 444)

Here we are, the Hindu race, whose vitality, whose life principle, whose very soul, as it were, is in religion. (III. 177)

The Hindu must not give up his religion, but must keep religion within its proper limits and give freedom to society to grow. (V. 22)

The whole religion of the Hindu is centred in realization. (I. 16)

The Hindu religion does not consist in struggles and attempts to believe a certain doctrine or dogma, but in realizing—not in believing, but in being and becoming. (I. 13)

The Hindus have to learn a little bit of materialism from the West and teach them a little bit of spirituality. (VI. 115)

Until the absence of jealousy and obedience to leaders are learnt by the Hindu, there will be no power of organization. (V. 216)

With all their faults the Hindus are head and shoulders above all other nations in morality and spirituality. (VIII. 322)

Hindu thinkers were as bold, and in some cases, much bolder than the moderns. (II. 90)

The race that produced Sita—if it only dreamt of her has a reverence for woman that is unmatched on the earth. (V. 231)

No religion on earth preaches the dignity of humanity in such a lofty strain as Hinduism, and no religion on earth treads upon the necks of the poor and the low in such a fashion as Hinduism. (V. 15)

Hinduism indicates one duty, only one, for the human soul. It is to seek to realize the permanent amidst the evanescent. (V. 232)

The old Hinduism can only be reformed through Hinduism, and not through the new-fangled reform movements. (VIII. 308)

**Holiness**

Whatever is old becomes holy. (II. 159)

So long as holiness is thus supremely venerated, India cannot die. (IV. 160)

Holiness is the greatest power. (VI. 89)

**Home**

East or West, home is best. (III. 309)

## Hope

Infinite hope begets infinite aspiration. (III. 445)

## Householder

The householder is the centre of life and society. (I. 46)

The householder is the basis, the prop, of the whole society. (I. 45)

## Humanity

Humanity travels not from error to truth, but from truth to truth. (IV. 147)

Every human being is a perfect being. (II. 502)

Human nature is very conservative. (II. 316)

## Idea

Almost every good idea in this world can be carried to a disgusting extreme. (III. 67)

In *Shabda* or idea, all gross objects have their subtle forms. (VI. 497)

## Ideal

The ideal of man is to see God in everything. (II. 152)

We must have an ideal. (II. 63)

Without the struggle towards the Infinite there can be no ideal. (II. 63)

We must even have the highest ideal. (II. 152)

Our ideal is the Brahmin of spiritual culture and renunciation. (III. 197)

It is a great thing to take up a grand ideal in life and then give up one's whole life to it. (III. 168)

Every person projects his or her own ideal on the outside world and kneels before it. (III. 90)

The life of the practical is in the ideal. (IV. 286)

It is the ideal that has made us what we are, and will make us what we are going to be. (IV. 285)

The power of the ideal is in the practical. (IV. 286)

Live for an ideal, and that one ideal alone. (V. 251)

That is the one great first step—the real desire for the ideal. (V. 252)

There is only one ideal in morality unselfishness. (IV. 150)

The highest ideal is always selfless. (VI. 143)

The highest ideal is eternal and entire self-abnegation, where there is no 'I', but all is 'Thou'. (I. 84-5)

## Idleness

Nothing is done by leading idle lives. (VI. 298)

The real evil is idleness, which is the principal cause of our poverty. (V. 375)

## Idolatry

We are all born idolaters, and idolatry is good, because it is in the nature of man. (II. 40)

## Imitations

Even if an imitation is good, it is never genuine. (I. 483)

Imitation is not civilization. (III. 381)

Imitation, cowardly imitation, never makes for progress. (III. 381)

## Immortality

You are immortal only when you are the whole. (III. 417)

What is strong and invigorating is immortal. (IV. 407)

The idea of immortality is inherent in man. (II. 32)

Immortality and bliss are not to be acquired, we possess them already; they have been ours all the time. (II. 350)

By renunciation alone immortality was reached. (IV. 338)

To talk of immortality in constantly changing things is absurd. (II. 81)

## Impermanence

No permanent or everlasting good can be done to the world. (I. 111)

Whatever is weak and corrupt is liable to die—what are we to do with it ? (IV. 406-07)

Decadence seizes everything in this life. (I. 247)

Everything that is the result of combination must get dissolved and die. (III. 84)

Everything mutable is a compound. (I. 7)

Everything compound must undergo that change which is called destruction. (I. 7)

All combinations must dissolve. (I. 494)

All the heavens and the world are in the person. (I. 495)

Not one is constant, but everything is changing, matter eternally concreting and disintegrating. (I. 151)

The whole world is going towards death; everything dies. (II. 92)

Everything is evanescent. (II. 71)

Every particle in this body is continually changing. (II. 440)

Everything in nature is constantly changing. (II. 440)

Ours are only sand, and, therefore, the building comes down with a crash in no time. (III. 430)

This world is a delusion of two days. (III. 148)

Everyone has to die, the saint or the sinner, the rich or the poor. (III. 431)

No dream can be eternal; it must end sooner or later. (VI. 68)

There is none who can keep his dream for ever. (VI. 68)

Everything born must die. (II. 177)

The body is subject to the law of growth and decay; what grows must of necessity decay. (IV. 188)

Everything that has a beginning in time must end in time. (III. 124)

This life comes and goes—wealth, fame, enjoyments are only of a few days. (V. 114)

Enjoyment, misery, luxury, wealth, power, and poverty, even life itself, are all evanescent. (II. 71)

Birth, growth, development, decay, death—this is the sequence in all nature. (VI. 41)

Life is not eternal. (VI. 419)

Change is inherent in every form. (VI. 20)

Nothing is to last for ever. (VI. 419)

All prosperity which comes with Mammon is transient, is only for a moment. (VIII. 213)

Everyone, everything is gone, is going, and will go. (VIII. 148)

Nothing in this relative world can be eternal. (VIII. 251)

Nothing external can be eternal. (VIII. 251)

Name and form come and go, but substance remains ever the same. (VIII. 247)

Excepting the infinite spirit, everything else is changing. (IV. 249)

'Everything is evanescent, everything is changeful'— knowing this, the sage gives up both pleasure and pain and becomes a witness of this panorama (the universe) without attaching himself to anything. (VIII. 344)

## Impurity

If you think yourselves impure, impure you will be. (III. 130)

We cannot see impurity without having it inside ourselves. (II. 327)

Impurity is a mere superimposition under which your real nature has become hidden. (III. 159)

No impure soul can be religious. (IV. 24)

## India

There is only one country in the world which understands religion—it is India. (VIII. 322)

India's theme is religion. (V. 210)

India's heart must break, and the flow of spirituality will come out. (V. 210)

It (religion) is the backbone, the bed-rock, the foundation upon which the national edifice has been built. (III. 204)

With us, religion is the only ground along which we can move. (III. 314)

Religion is the one and sole interest of the people of India. (III. 178)

Religion is the peculiarity of the growth of the Indian mind. (III. 203)

To the Indian mind there is nothing higher than religious ideals. (III. 287)

The Indian mind is first religious, then anything else. (III. 289)

Here in India, it is religion that forms the very core of the national heart. (III. 204)

In religion lies the vitality of India. (IV. 324)

For good or for evil, the religious ideal has been flowing into India for thousands of years; for good or for evil, the Indian atmosphere has been filled with ideals of religion for shining scores of centuries; for good or for evil, we have been born and brought up in the very midst of these ideas of religion, till it has entered into our very blood and tingled with every drop in our veins, and has become one with our constitution, become the very vitality of our lives. (III. 178-79)

Religion and religion alone is the life of India, and when that goes India will die, in spite of politics, in spite of social reforms, in spite of Kubera's wealth poured upon the head of every one of her children. (III. 146)

Each nation has a main current in life; in India it is religion. (IV. 373)

This is the line of life, this is the line of growth, and this is the line of well-being in India—to follow the track of religion. (III. 179)

Here in this blessed land, the foundation, the backbone, the life-centre is religion and religion alone. (III. 148)

This our motherland, has religion and religion alone for its basis, for its backbone, for the bed-rock upon which the whole building of its life has been based. (III. 177)

India is the land of religion. (IV. 322)

Our vigour, our strength, nay, our national life is in our religion. (III. 289)

Here in India, religion is the one and the only occupation of life. (III. 107)

In India, religious life forms the centre, the keynote of the whole music of national life. (III. 220)

Religion is the life of India, religion is the language of this country, the symbol of all its movements. (IV. 462)

Our vitality is concentrated in our religion. (III. 178)

Renunciation, that is the flag, the banner of India, floating over the world, the one undying thought which India sends again and again as a warning to dying races, as a warning to all tyranny, as a warning to wickedness in the world. (III. 344)

Religion, in India, means realization and nothing short of that. (III. 377)

All history of Indian life is the struggle for the realization of the ideal of the Vedanta through good or bad fortune. (V. 217)

We have no quarrel with any religion in the world, whether it teaches men to worship Christ, Buddha, or Mohammed or any other prophet. (III. 132)

National union in India must be a gathering up of its scattered spiritual forces. (III. 371)

In India religion was never shackled. (IV. 346)

The search after the universal is the one search of Indian philosophy and religion. (III. 81)

Religion in India must be made as free and as easy of access as is God's air. (III. 383)

Religion in India culminates in freedom. (VIII. 221)

We all hold in India that the soul is by its nature pure and perfect, infinite in power and blessed. (III. 375)

All the orthodox systems of Indian philosophy have one goal in view, the liberation of the soul through perfection. (I. 122)

India is the only place where, with all its faults, the soul finds its freedom, its God. (VI. 359)

The gift of India is the gift of religion and philosophy, and wisdom and spirituality. (III. 273)

Renunciation and spirituality are the two great ideas of India. (II. 372)

This nation still lives; the *raison d'être* is it still holds to God, to the treasure-house of religion and spirituality. (III. 148)

Here in India the first and the foremost duty of our lives is to be spiritual first, and then, if there is time, let others things come. (III. 371)

India's contribution to the sum total of human knowledge has been spirituality, philosophy. (III. 171)

Whether you believe in spirituality or not, for the sake of the national life, you have to get a hold on spirituality and keep to it. (III. 153)

Modern India belongs to the spiritual part of the Vedas. (III. 536)

India's gift to the world is the light spiritual. (III. 109)

A nation in India must be a union of those whose hearts beat to the same spiritual tune. (III. 371)

India is still living; who says she is dead? (III. 165)

India dies not. (III. 444)

The Indian nation cannot be killed. (IV. 160)

Political greatness or military power is never the mission of our race; it never was, and, mark my words, it never will be. (III. 108)

India is India. (V. 210)

To Europeanize India is therefore an impossible and foolish task. (V. 198)

India can never be Europe until she dies. (IV. 347)

In the midst of all our misery, our poverty, and degeneration, the heart beats as warm as of yore, when the 'wealth of Ind' was the proverb of nations and India was the land of the 'Aryan'. (V. 122)

Thou blessed land of the Aryas, thou wast never degraded. (IV. 314)

We have to give back to the nation its lost individuality and *raise the masses*. (VI. 255)

The only hope of India is from the masses. (V. 106)

India must rise, the masses and the poor are to be made happy. (V. 35)

No amount of politics would be of any avail until the masses in India are once more well-educated, well-fed, and well cared for. (V. 222-23)

The one thing that is at the root of all evils in India is the condition of the poor. (IV. 362)

Nowhere has activity been more pronounced than in this blessed land of ours. (III. 137-38)

If we want to regenerate India, we must work for them (masses). (V. 223)

What our country now wants are muscles of iron and nerves of steel, gigantic wills which nothing can resist, which can penetrate into the mysteries and the secrets of the universe, and will accomplish their purpose in any fashion even if it meant going down to the bottom of the ocean and meeting death face to face. (III. 190)

She is awakening, this motherland of ours, from her deep long sleep. (III. 146)

The present want of India is the *Kshatriya* force. (V. 316)

India sets the example of real strength, that is meek-ness. (V. 190)

What India wants is a new electric fire to stir up a fresh vigour in the national veins. (V. 57)

India's potentialities are great and will be called forth. (V. 199)

On our work depends the coming of the India of the future. (III. 154)

None can resist her any more; never is she going to sleep any more; no outward powers can hold her back any more; for the infinite giant is rising to her feet. (III. 146)

India must conquer the world, and nothing less than that is my ideal. (III. 316)

We, of all nations of the world, have never been a conquering race, and that blessing is on our head, and therefore we live. (III. 106)

We have yet something to teach to the world. (III. 148)

I see in my mind's eye the future perfect India rising out of this chaos and strife, glorious and invincible, with Vedanta brain and Islam body. (VI. 416)

This idea of oneness is the great lesson India has to give. (III. 160)

We are destined by the Lord to do great things in India. (V. 13)

Here alone is the best ideal for mankind. (III. 138)

The Indian nation never stood for imperial glory. Wealth and power, then, were not the ideals of the race. (VIII. 74)

India is still the first and foremost of all the nations of the world. (III. 147)

The talk of the brotherhood of man becomes in India the brotherhood of universal life, of animals, and of all life down to the little ants—all these are our bodies. (III. 126)

You are the descendants of the *Devas*. (IV. 352)

If we are to live at all, we must be a scientific nation. (VI. 113)

The ideal woman in India is the mother, the mother first, and the mother last. (VIII. 57)

In India, father and mother are living gods to their children. (II. 158)

The Indian people are intensely socialistic. (III. 516)

They are ... tremendously individualistic. (III. 516)

The one great lesson, therefore, that the world wants most, that the world has yet to learn from India, is the idea not only of toleration, but of sympathy. (III. 114)

Priestcraft is the bane of India. (IV. 327)

There is no *polytheism* in India. (I. 15)

The characteristic of my nation is this transcenden-talism, this struggle to go beyond, this daring to tear the veil off the face of nature and have at any risk, at any price, a glimpse of the beyond. (III. 149)

The one characteristic of Indian thought is its silence, its calmness. (III. 274)

Gratitude and hospitality are the peculiar characteristics of Indian humanity. (V. 122)

The Indian ideal is not to go to heaven. (VI. 57)

I discard the idea that India was ever passive. (III. 137)

Here in India, everybody wants to become a leader, and there is nobody to obey. (V. 216)

To do something conjointly is not in our very national character. (VI. 323)

## Individuality

That is the real individuality, when there is no more division, and no more parts. (II. 419)

## Jealousy

That man is not humble or loving who is jealous. (VI. 145)

Jealousy is the root of all evil, and a most difficult thing to conquer. (IV. 6)

Jealousy is the bane of our race. (V. 99)

Jealousy is the bane of our national character. (IV. 359-60)

We cannot give up jealousy and rally together. That is our national sin ! (VI. 256)

Jealousy is the central vice of every enslaved race. (V. 56)

Jealousy is a terrible, horrible sin; it enters a man so mysteriously. (VI. 145)

## Jivanmukta

He is *Jivanmukta* who can live in this world without being attached. (III. 10)

It is all 'here'. To live and move in god—even here, even in this body ! (VIII. 219)

## Judge

We must not judge of higher things from a low standpoint. (III. 3)

Each man is to be judged by his own idea each race by its own standard and ideal, each custom of each country by its own reasoning and conditions. (V. 241)

## Kali

This Kali is Brahman in manifestation. (VII. 229)

## Kama

*Kama* (lust) is blind and leads to hell. (VI. 116)

## Kama-kanchana

The renunciation of *Kama-kanchana* is the most important. (V. 261)

## Kapila

There is no philosophy in the world that is not indebted to Kapila. (II. 445)

Wherever there is any attempt at psychology or philosophy, the great father of it is this man, Kapila. (II. 455)

Wherever there is any philosophy or rational thought, it owes something or other to Kapila. (II. 455)

## Knowledge

Pleasure is not the goal of man, but knowledge. (I. 27)

Knowledge is the goal of all life. (IV. 210)

We are all of us struggling towards knowledge. (I. 204)

The real life of man consists of knowledge. (I. 52)

He who can become mad with an idea, he alone sees light. (I. 177)

All our knowledge is based upon experience. (I. 125)

Instinct, reason, and inspiration are the three instruments of knowledge. (II. 389)

Generalization is the essence of knowledge. (IV. 380)

Books are infinite in number, and time is short; therefore the secret of knowledge is to take what is essential. (I. 236)

Perception is our only real knowledge or religion. (VII. 59)

It is practice first, and knowledge afterwards. (II. 317)

All knowledge depends upon calmness of mind. (VII. 72)

'No knowledge is possible without a teacher.' (IV. 431)

No one can teach anybody. (V. 366)

The gift of knowledge is the highest gift in the world. (VII. 256)

The first end of life is knowledge; the second end of life is happiness. (VI. 83)

Knowledge and happiness lead to freedom. (VI. 83)

No action can give you freedom; only knowledge can make you free, Knowledge is irresistible; the mind cannot take it or reject it. (VII. 54)

Knowledge itself is a manufactured something, a combination; it is not reality. (I. 213)

Knowledge itself is the highest reward of knowledge. (I. 130)

Knowledge alone can make us perfect. (VII. 38)

Knowledge is power. (I. 144)

The only value of knowledge is in the strengthening, the disciplining, of the mind. (VI. 64)

Is there a greater strength than that of knowledge? (VI. 325)

Knowledge is objectification. (II. 134)

Knowledge is a limitation, knowledge is objectifying. (II. 82)

Knowledge is, as it were, a lower step, a degeneration. (II. 82)

All knowledge must stand on perception of certain facts, and upon that we have to build our reasoning. (II. 162)

All human knowledge proceeds out of experience; we cannot know anything except by experience. (II. 226)

All knowledge is by reaction. (II. 458)

All knowledge and all power are within and not without. (I. 422)

Nobody ever created knowledge; man brings it from within. (II. 339)

There is no knowledge in nature; all knowledge comes from the human soul. (I. 422)

All knowledge is within us. (I. 412)

All knowledge is within (the) mind. (I. 509)

Knowledge is God. (VIII. 137)

All this knowledge is God himself. (VIII. 137)

Just as creation is infinite and eternal, without beginning and without end, so is the knowledge of God without beginning and without end. (III. 119)

Higher knowledge is thus clearly shown to be the knowledge of the Brahman. (III. 85)

In real knowledge there is no touch of work. (VII. 212)

Knowledge means finding this unity. (III. 5)

Knowledge is nothing but finding unity in the midst of diversity. (III. 397)

Illumination born of discriminative reflection is the ultimate aim of Upanishadic knowledge. (VI. 507)

All knowledge is Veda, infinite as God is infinite. (VIII. 136)

All human knowledge is but a part of religion. (VII. 103)

Knowledge realizes one. (IV. 233)

Knowing does not mean simply intellectual assent, it means realization. (II. 410)

There is nothing higher than this knowledge of the Atman; all else is Maya, mere jugglery. (VI. 519)

Knowledge does not come by sacrifice, but by seeking, worshipping, knowing the Atman. (VII. 42)

The goal of all is the knowledge of the Self, the realization of this Self. (VI. 457)

There is no other way to the knowledge of the Self but
through *Sannyasa*. (VI. 506-07)

All other kinds of knowledge are but non-knowledge in
comparison with Self-knowledge. (IV. 404)

When we know that we are the Self, then we are
free. (VI. 84)

Spiritual knowledge is the only thing that can destroy
our miseries for ever. (I. 52)

Spiritual knowledge can only be given in silence like
the dew that falls unseen and unheard, yet bringing
into bloom masses of roses. (III. 222)

Of what use is knowledge if it does not show us the way
to the Highest? (IV. 281)

Supreme knowledge (can be learnt) even from the man
of low birth. (IV. 338)

The gross melts into the fine, physics into metaphysics,
in every department of knowledge. (III. 3)

All knowledge is in the soul. (I. 514)

The soul does not know, It is knowledge itself. (I. 249)

Whatever we know we have to know in and through Him.
(II. 133)

Knowledge was not in matter, it was in man all the
time. (II. 339)

Within man is all knowledge. (V. 366)

It is only discovered—what was covered is un-
covered. (VIII. 136)

Knowledge exists, man only discovers it. (VII. 79)

Knowledge can never be created, it can only be
discovered; and every man who makes a great
discovery is inspired. (VII. 39)

Infinite knowledge abides within everyone in the fullest measure. (VIII. 137)

Past, present, and future knowledge, all exist in all of us. (VIII. 136)

In knowledge is worship. (II. 335)

To separate ourselves utterly from matter and all belief in its reality is true *Jnana*. (VIII. 5)

No one who sells his knowledge is an *Apta*. (I. 205)

The *Jnani* has to be free from all forms. (VIII. 11)

The *Jnani* is a tremendous rationalist; he denies everything. (VIII. 11)

All over the world, it is the wise man who enjoys the happiness of the world. (III. 20)

All wise men think alike. (VIII. 160)

The *Jnani* takes nothing for granted. (VIII. 11)

*Jnana-yoga* is the surest way of arriving at facts. (VI. 42)

## Language

Language must be made like pure steel—turn and twist it any way you like, it is again the same—it cleaves a rock in twain at one stroke, without its edge being turned. (VI. 187-88)

Language is the vehicle of ideas. (VI. 188)

(Now) Human language is the attempt to express the truth that is within. (II. 73)

## Law

Law is uniform. (I. 197)

Law is death. (III. 516)

Interdependence is the law of the whole universe. (II. 132)

All love is life, it is the only law of life; all selfishness is
   death, and this is true here or hereafter. (IV. 367)
Too many laws are a sure sign of death. (V. 287)
All things in nature work according to law. (VI. 92)
A law is that which cannot be broken. (VI. 100)
All nature is bound by law, the law of its own action;
   and this law can never be broken. (VI. 99)
Law exists so long as we are ignorant. (VI. 84)
Evil actions leave none scot-free; Mother never spares
   anybody. (VIII. 499)
Yesterday, competition was the law. Today, co-operation
   is the law. Tomorrow there is no law. (VIII. 223)
The eternal law is self-sacrifice, not self-assertion. (VIII. 23)
The law of *Karma* is the law of causation. (VI. 92)

## Leader

It is a very difficult task to take on the role of a
   leader. (VI. 284)
The leaders of our societies have never been either
   generals or kings, but *Rishis*. (III. 175)
There is no allegiance possible where there is no
   character in the leader, and perfect purity ensures
   the most lasting allegiance and confidence.
There must not be a shade of jealousy or selfishness,
   then you are a leader. (VI. 284)
First, by birth, and secondly, unselfish—that's a
   leader. (VI. 284)
A leader must be impersonal. (VIII. 429)
Not everyone is *born to lead*. (VIII. 428)
The best leader, however, is one who 'leads like the
   baby'. (VIII. 428)

## Learning

We have to learn from others. (III. 381)

We have indeed many things to learn from others. (III. 381)

He who adjusts himself best lives the longest. (VI. 110)

It is learning and intellect that keep things sure. (I. 349)

If a man reads but one word of love, he indeed becomes learned. (IV. 20)

## Liberation

There is no liberation in getting powers. (I. 211)

Liberation means entire freedom—freedom from the bondage of good, as well as from the bondage of evil. (I. 55)

Liberation consists in knowing our unity with the wonderful Impersonality. (III. 129)

What avails it all to have only one's own liberations ! (VI. 502)

Liberation is only for him who gives up everything for others. (VI. 395)

Liberty of both soul and body is to be striven for. (VI. 86)

*Liberty, Mukti,* is all my religion, and everything that tries to curb it, I will avoid by fight or flight. (V. 72)

## Life

The first manifest effect of life is expansion. (III. 272)

The sign of life is expansion. (III. 316)

Expansion is the sign of life, and we must spread over the world with our spiritual ideals. (IV. 486)

The sign of life is strength and growth. (I. 479)

Life is a series of fights and disillusionments. (V. 150)

The great benefit in this life is struggle. (V. 252)

Struggle is the sign of life. (VII. 219)

The (life) is a battlefield, fight your way out. (VIII. 227)

It is the variety that is the source of life, the sign of life. (IV. 127)

It is impossible that all difference can cease; it must exist; without variation life must cease. (III. 115)

Variety is the very soul of life. (III. 131)

The highest use of life is to hold it at the service of all beings. (III. 84)

Our whole life is a contradiction, a mixture of existence and non-existence. (II. 91)

A perfect life is a contradiction in terms. (I. 84)

The present life is of five minutes. (III. 148)

Life is but a dream of death. (VI. 93)

No more is there life, therefore no more is there death. (III. 128)

Life is too short to be spent in talking about frauds and cranks. (V. 65)

Immortal life is a contradiction in terms, for life, being a compound, cannot be immortal. (VI. 45)

Whoever gives up this life for His sake, finds the life immortal. (IV. 149)

When you give life, you will have life. (III. 273)

None can live in the world without resistance, without destruction, without desire. (V. 125)

The secret of life is to give and take. (III. 317)

It is the *life* that is the highest and the only way to stir the hearts of people; it carries the personal magnetism. (V. 65)

Life is a product, a compound, and as such must resolve itself into its elements. (VII. 38)

Motion is life. (VII. 422)

Adaptibility is the whole mystery of life. (VI. 110)

Life to everyone must be a compromise. (VI. 372)

All the possibilities of life are in the germ. (II. 228)

He alone lives whose life is in the whole universe. (II. 80)

One touch, one glance, can change a whole life. (IV. 179)

Living is always slavery. (IV. 232)

Life is full of ills, the world is full of evils. (II. 144)

Life can only convey life. (II. 23)

Life has its shadow, death. (II. 177)

Life is another name for death, and death for life. (II. 234)

You come into life to accumulate. (II. 5)

This one life is the universal life, heavens and all those
    places are here. (II. 325)

Life is sweet, because it thinks of the Beloved. (III. 80)

All life is evil. (III. 214)

*Life is and must be accompanied by evil*. (VII. 12)

It is a change of the soul itself for the better that alone
    will cure the evils of life. (III. 182)

The one great lesson I was taught is that life is misery,
    nothing but misery. (V. 143-44)

The life of every man is, in a manner, the life of the past.
    (IV. 139)

The first thing necessary is a quiet and peaceable
    life. (V. 250)

We are lamps, and our burning is what we call
    'Life'. (VII. 38)

This life is a hard fact. (II. 182)

This life is a great chance. (VI. 262)

Life on the plane of the Spirit is the only life, life on any
    other plane is mere death. (V. 267)

Wherever there is life, the storehouse of infinite energy
is behind it. (I. 156)

The secret of life is not enjoyment, but education through
experience. (V. 150)

Life is but a playground, however gross the play may
be. (II. 402)

The whole of this life can be only described as a
gymnasium. (V. 267)

This world is just a gymnasium in which we play; our
life is an eternal holiday. (VII. 49)

It is a land of dreams; it does not matter whether one
enjoys or weeps; they are but dreams, and as such,
must break sooner or later. (VIII. 504)

Our whole life is continuous suffering. (VIII. 99)

Life is but a dream. (VIII. 504)

The perfect life would be a wonderful harmony between
doing and suffering. (VIII. 265)

Our difficulty in life is that we are guided by the present
and not by the future. (VIII. 414)

Life can only spring from life, thought from thought,
matter from matter. (VIII. 235)

This life is our teacher, and dying only makes room to
begin over again. (VIII. 18-19)

The object of life is to learn the laws of spiritual
progress. (IV. 190)

Life in this world is an attempt to see God. (VIII. 227)

The whole life is a succession of dreams. (V. 100)

It is the same light coming through glasses of different
colours. (I. 18)

Take the hands away and there is light; the light exists

always for us, the self-effulgent nature of the human soul. (II. 356)

Light comes gently, slowly, but surely it comes. (II. 403)

The vibration of light is everywhere. (II. 42)

Light must come. (IV. 127)

## Limitation

The limited is a mere fiction. (II. 305)

All friendship, all love, is only limitation. (V. 72)

Ceremonies, books, and forms—all these are links in the chain. (I. 439)

## Lord

The Lord Himself works incessantly and is ever without attachment. (I. 60)

Whatever comes to you is but the Lord, the Eternal, the Blessed One. (II. 326)

The Lord alone is true. (IV. 60)

The Lord is the only One who never changes. (IV. 129)

The Lord is the wealth of those who have nothing. (IV. 294)

Is not the Lord infinitely greater than all human help? (V. 57)

The Lord is great. I know He will help me. (V. 16)

It is the Lord who protects His children in the depths of the sea. (V. 51)

Glory unto the Lord, we will succeed. (V. 17)

Glory unto the Lord—march on, the Lord is our General. (V. 17)

Is the Lord to be hoodwinked by idle talk? (VI. 253)

The Lord provides everything. (VI. 284)

The goldness of gold, the silverness of silver, the manhood of man, the womanhood of woman, the reality of everything is the Lord. (VI. 378)

The will of Vishweshwara, the Lord of the universe, will prevail—whatever that may be. (VIII. 283-84)

Seek the Lord and getting Him we get all. (VIII. 27)

The Lord is all blissfulness. (VIII. 134)

Only the Lord is unchangeable and He is Love. (VIII. 400)

He, the Lord of the universe, is in every one. (VIII. 135)

## Loss

He who is always afraid of loss always loses. (VIII. 433)

## Love

Love is the easiest and smoothest way towards the self-surrender or subjection of the will, and hatred, the opposite. (VI. 378-79)

Love is beyond time and space, it is absolute. (VII. 11)

Love itself is the eternal, endless sacrifice. (VI. 76)

Love is its own end. (VI. 71)

Love can never be the means: it must be the perfect end. (VI. 71)

Love is always of the ideal. (VIII. 222)

Love is struggle of a human Soul to find its complement its stable equilibrium its infinite rest. (V. 426)

Love is, therefore, the only law of life. (VI. 320)

Love is always the highest ideal. (II. 49)

The perfect love is very rare in human relation. (VI. 144)

This (love) is the one motive power in the universe. (II. 51)

Love is the only form in which love is loved. (VIII. 154)

Love knows no bargaining. (III. 87)

The only medium through which spiritual force can be transmitted is love. (III. 51)

There is only one element in life which is worth having at any cost, and it is love. (V. 144)

All hatred is 'Killing the self by the self'; therefore, love is the law of life. (VIII. 35)

Love is the easiest of all, it waits for no logic, it is natural. (VII. 10)

There are no 'rights', all is love. (VIII. 23)

Love opens the most impossible gates; love is the gate to all the secrets of the universe. (III. 225)

Love alone is the fittest thing to survive and not hatred. (III. 188)

Love was the most visible of all visible things. (III. 392)

Whether we do good or evil, the propeller is love. (III. 365)

All earthly love proceeds from the body. (V. 138)

Where love is not returned for love, cold indifference is the natural result. (III. 86)

Mother represents colourless love that knows no barter, love that never dies. (VI. 149)

Every act of love brings happiness. (I. 57)

Real love makes us unattached. (I. 58)

Unattached love will not hurt you. (I. 442)

Love matter and you become matter. (I. 499)

If you love, that love will come back to you, completing the circle. (I. 196)

*Prema* is love, it leads to heaven. (VI. 116)

The last and highest manifestation of *Prana* is love. (VI. 129)

We only love that which understands love, that which draws our love. (VI. 51)

Pure love has no motive. (VI. 90)

Kindness and love can buy you the whole world. (VI. 404)

None lives, my boys, but he who loves. (IV. 367)

We must love all. (IV. 221)

Love, Love—that's the one thing, the sole treasure. (IV. 494)

The real help is feeling, love. (II. 307)

Salvation is in work and love. (VIII. 240)

The way of all ways to realization is love. (VIII. 258)

In the highest love, union is only of the spirit. (VIII. 221)

Love immense and infinite, broad as the sky and deep as the ocean—this is the one great gain in life. Blessed is he who gets it. (V. 144)

Good results can be produced only through love, through sympathy. (III. 198)

The love of the whole includes the love of the parts. (III. 92)

None but men of great renunciation, none but mighty giants among men, have a right to that Love Divine. (V. 345)

When love comes method dies. (V. 426)

Every step that has been really gained in the world has been gained by love. (VII. 28)

Love cannot be without a subject and an object. (VIII. 153)

Merely to love is the sole request that true love has to ask. (VIII. 201)

Love shall win the victory. (V. 51)

Love makes no distinction between man and man. (V. 78)

Love makes the whole universe as one's own home. (V. 78)

Matter changed into spirit by the force of love. (VIII. 429)

Love never fails. (V. 51)

Love never dies. (VIII. 386)

The only worship is love. (VIII. 331)

Love comes and penetrates through the forms and sees beyond. (VI. 143)

Love conquers in the long run. (VI. 284)

It is love that gives you the supernatural powers, love that gives you *Bhakti*, love that gives illumination, and love, again, that leads to emancipation. (VI. 401)

Love banishes all fear. (VIII. 154)

Love knows no fear. (VI. 71)

Love questions not. (VI. 70)

Love loves for the sake of love itself. (VIII. 154)

Therefore love for love's sake, because it is the only law of life, just as you breathe to live. (VI. 320)

Love itself is the highest recompense of love. (II. 393)

Love is always the giver and never the taker. (II. 48)

Love knows no reward. (III. 88)

Love is always for love's sake. (III. 88)

My nature is to love Him, and therefore I love. (I. 12)

To love because it is the nature of love to love is undeniably the highest and the most unselfish manifestation of love that may be seen in the world. (III. 86)

The first sign of love is when love asks nothing, (when it) gives everything. (VI. 70)

Love never asks, never begs. (VIII. 154)

Begging is not the language of love. (III. 88)

There is not true love possible in the slave. (I. 57)

Beggar's love is no love at all. (VI. 70)

The first test of love is that it knows no bargaining. (II. 48)

The reward of love is love. (II. 53)

Ordinarily human love is seen to flourish only in places where it is returned. (III. 86)

*Prema* cannot come while there is lust. (V. 346)

Lust is the death of love. (V. 426)

There can be no love so long as there is lust—even a speck of it, as it were, in the heart. (V. 345)

With love, there is no painful reaction. (I. 58)

There is no act of love which does not bring peace and blessedness as its reaction. (I. 57-58)

Love only brings a reaction of bliss. (I. 58)

Love is always a manifestation of bliss. (VIII. 276)

It requires no proofs to demonstrate the existence of the beloved to the lover. (III. 91-92)

To the lover the beloved is the most beautiful being that ever existed. (II. 49)

Love is simply an expression of this infinite unity. (VIII. 238)

Love binds, love makes for that oneness. (II. 304)

The Infinite One comes within my fist under the bondage of love. (VI. 259)

All this is the manifestation of that One Love more or less expressed. (II. 304)

If one would expand, he must love, and when he ceases to love he dies. (II. 500)

The highest expression of love is unification. (VII. 30)

It is indeed very difficult to have an equal love for all, but without it there is no *Mukti*. (VI. 357)

With the love of God will come, as its effect, the love of every one in the long run. (VIII. 258)

'As oil poured from one vessel to another falls in an unbroken line, so, when the mind in an unbroken stream thinks of the Lord, we have what is called *Para-Bhakti* or supreme love.' (III. 85)

Love must get to its right destination, it must go unto Him, who is really the infinite ocean of love. (III. 97)

Our love must, therefore, be given to the Highest One who never dies and never changes, to Him in the ocean of whose love there is neither ebb nor flow. (III. 97)

Wherever there is love, it is He. (II. 393)

Love is existence, God Himself; and all this is the manifestation of that One Love, more or less expressed. (II. 304)

The Love of God is the only love that is higher than a mother's love; all others are lower. (I. 68)

Nothing must stand between me and God except love. (VI. 76)

Gopi-Lila (his disport with the cowherd maids) is the acme of the religion of love in which individuality vanishes and there is communion. (VI. 110)

When a person loves the Lord, the whole universe becomes dear to him, because it is all His. (III. 81)

Men who cannot love God are no good, whatever work they do. (I. 513)

Highest love for God can never be achieved without renunciation. (VI. 505)

## Machines

Machines never made mankind happy and never will make. (IV. 155)

## Man

Man is divine. (II. 193)

Man is the highest being in creation, because he attains to freedom. (II. 258)

Man is the greatest of all beings. (V. 94)

Man is the nearest approach to Brahman. (II. 258)

Man is the greatest being that ever can be. (VII. 76)

Man is the highest being that exists, and this is the greatest world. (VII. 30)

Man is the apex of the only world we can ever know. (VII. 31)

Man is the epitome of all things and all knowledge is in him. (VIII. 21)

Man is the best mirror, and the purer the man, the more clearly he can reflect God. (VIII. 26)

Man in his true nature is substance, soul, spirit. (VIII. 247)

Man has infinite power within himself, and he can realize it—he can realize himself as the one infinite Self. (VIII. 101-02)

Man as Atman is really free; as man he is bound, changed by every physical condition. (VII. 38)

Each man is perfect by his nature; prophets have manifested this perfection, but it is potential in us. (VII. 97)

Man always *is* perfect or he never could become so. (VIII. 14)

Man is a compound of animality, humanity and divinity. (V. 417)

In one sense Brahman is known to every human being; he knows, 'I am'; but man does not know himself as he is. (VII. 34)

*Man is man so long as he is struggling to rise above nature*, and this nature is both internal and external. (II. 64-65)

The Real Man, therefore, is one and infinite, the omnipresent Spirit. (II. 78)

Man is a degeneration of what he was. (II. 72)

Man cannot always think of matter, however pleasurable it may be. (II. 64)

The perfect man sees nothing but God. (II. 50)

There is no end to the power a man can obtain. (II. 20)

Man can become like God. (II. 33)

Man alone becomes *God*. (V. 94)

Man is a creature who thinks. (III. 359)

Man is the product of two forces, action and reaction, which make him think. (III. 359)

*Manushya* (man) is a being with *Manas* (mind). (III. 359)

Man can think of divine things only in his own human way; to us the Absolute can be expressed only in our relative language. (III. 93)

Man is the only animal that naturally looks upwards; every other animal naturally looks down. (III. 3)

There are three things in the make-up of man. There is the body, there is the mind, and there is the soul. (V. 463-64)

Infinite perfection is in every man, though unmani-fested. (IV. 437)

We are all called 'man' because we are the progeny of Manu. (II. 73)

The glory of man is that he is a thinking being. (II. 336)

The happiest is the man who is not at all selfish. (II. 465)

The ignorant man never enjoys. (III. 20)

The selfish man is the most miserable in the world. (II. 465)

Man is really free, the real man cannot but be free. (II. 282-83)

As long as a man thinks, this struggle must go on, and so long man must have some form of religion. (III. 1)

Man never dies, nor is he ever born; bodies die, but he never dies. (V. 411)

Man dies but once. (V. 87)

Man, therefore, according to the Vedanta philosophy, is the greatest being that is in the universe. (II. 271)

Each man has a mission in life, which is the result of all his infinite past *Karma*. (III. 152)

Man cannot go beyond his nature, no more than you can jump out of your body. (VIII. 299)

Man is not mind, he is soul. (VI. 35)

Man cannot be satisfied by wealth. (II. 161)

Man the infinite dreamer, dreaming finite dreams! (VIII. 251)

The real man is the one Unit Existence. (II. 280)

The apparent man is only a limitation of that Real Man. (II. 78)

The animal man lives in the senses. (II. 96)

That is why purity and morality have been always the object of religion; a pure, moral man has control of himself. (II. 17)

Man cannot live upon words, however he may try. (I. 140)

Man will have to go beyond intellect in the end. (I. 413)

Man is greater than the gods. (I. 400)

Only man makes *Karma*. (I. 399)

An intellectual, heartless man never becomes an inspired man. (I. 413)

Each man must begin where he stands, must learn how to control the things that are nearest to him. (I. 149)

Every human being has the right to ask the reason, why, and to have his question answered by himself, if he only takes the trouble. (I. 131)

Great occasions rouse even the lowest of human beings to some kind of greatness, but he alone is the really great man whose character is great always, the same wherever he be. (I. 29)

Man's experience in the world is to enable him to get out of its whirlpool. (I. 99)

The calm man is not the man who is dull. (I. 202)

Never say any man is hopeless. (I. 208)

Man is guided by the stomach. (I. 454)

Each human being stands for the divine. (I. 388)

Man is higher than all animal, than all angels; none is greater than man. (I. 142)

There is, however, one great danger in human nature, viz that man never examines himself. (I. 66)

No man was ever born who could stop his body one moment from changing. (I. 142)

Every human being has the right and the power to seek for religion. (I. 131)

Man is only apparently a person, but in reality he is the Impersonal Being. (II. 192)

The two phases of this distinction in life are—first, that the man who knows the real Self, will not be affected by anything; secondly, that that man alone can do good to the world. (V. 285)

That man alone who is the lord of his mind can become happy, and none else. (IV. 155)

Every man has in him the potentiality of attaining to perfect saintliness. (IV. 437)

Man is born to conquer nature. (IV. 155)

No man is ever satisfied. (IV. 240)

Man alone is blest with power to fight and conquer Fate, transcending bounds and laws. (IV. 386)

Man must raise himself to that higher plane if he wants to enjoy its beauties, to bathe in its light, to feel his life pulsating in unison with the Cause-Life of the universe. (IV. 284-85)

Man must realize God even in this life. (IV. 342)

Man must love others because those others are him-self. (VII. 96)

The worst, most demoniacal man has some virtues which the greatest saint has not; and the lowest worm may have certain things which the highest man has not. (III. 158)

As soon as his thinking-power goes, he becomes no better than an animal. (III. 359)

We have indeed many things to learn from others; yea, that man who refuses to learn is already dead. (III. 381)

The true *man* is he who is strong as strength itself and yet possesses a woman's heart. (III. 448)

A man who does the lower work is not, for that reason only, a lower man than he who does the higher works; a man should not be judged by the nature of his duties, but by the manner in which he does them. (V. 239)

It is man that makes everything, what can money do? (VI. 406)

Men talk and talk. (II. 474)

Man is very short-sighted and impatient. (VI. 136)

'Man is God, he is Narayana'. (VI. 319)

Man is made up of three qualities—brutal, human, and godly. (VI. 112)

Man is individual and at the same time universal. (VI. 121)

Man cannot get at Truth by external methods. (VI. 41)

Man is infinite, and this limitation in which he exists now is not his nature. (VI. 22)

Man is first to be saved; he must be given food, education, and spirituality. (VI. 451)

Men we want, the more you get, the better. (VI. 406)

There is no knowledge without experience, and man has to see God in his own soul. (VI. 133)

The man who is perfectly moral has nothing more to do; he is free. (VI. 126)

Man can only think of his ideal as a human being. (VII. 192)

Man has got this body simply to realize Self-know-ledge. (VII. 212)

Man longs for a concrete symbol, otherwise his heart is not satisfied. (VII. 276)

No man should be judged by his defects. (VII. 78)

As soon as a man or a nation loses faith, death comes. (VIII. 228)

When a man is under the control of his senses, he is of this world. (VIII. 227)

Every religion and every creed recognizes man as divine. (VIII. 199)

Man-manifestation is the highest in the phenomenal world. (V. 284)

The brotherhood of man is the much-to-be-desired end. (VIII. 199)

The perfect man is the highest reflection of that Being who is both subject and object. (III. 8)

The real spiritual man is broad everywhere. (V. 60)

The highest men cannot work, for in them there is no attachment. (I. 106)

The highest men are calm, silent, and unknown. (I. 106)

The highest kind of men silently collect true and noble ideas. (I. 105)

The highest men do not seek to get any name or fame from their knowledge. (I. 105)

Silently they (the highest men) live and silently they pass away. (I. 105)

The history of the world is the history of persons like Buddha and Jesus. (VIII. 226)

No man is to be judged by the mere nature of his duties, but all should be judged by the manner and the spirit in which they perform them. (I. 66)

It is an insult to a starving people to offer them religion; it is an insult to a starving man to teach him metaphysics. (I. 20)

Man is like an infinite spring, coiled up in a small box, and that spring is trying to unfold itself. (I. 389)

This human body is the greatest body in the universe, and a human being is the greatest being. (I. 142)

Man is to become divine by realizing the divine. (I. 16)

Man is not travelling from error to truth, but from truth to truth, from lower to higher truth. (I. 17)

Man's present state is a degeneration. (I. 197)

The greatest men in the world have passed away unknown. (I. 105)

This world is neither good nor evil; each man manufactures a world for himself. (I. 75)

Man alone attains to perfection, not even the Devas. (I. 142)

Each man is only a conduit for the infinite ocean of knowledge and power that lies behind mankind. (I. 122)

However much their systems of philosophy and religion may differ, all mankind stand in reverence and awe before the man who is ready to sacrifice himself for others. (I. 86)

Wherever there is a being, that being contains the infinite message of the Most High. (I. 424)

Actions must come when the man is there; the effect is bound to follow the cause. (II. 15)

A man can be of gigantic intellect, yet spiritually he may be a baby. (II. 40)

Man is not bound by any other laws excepting those which he makes for himself. (II. 348)

Man never progresses from error to truth, but from truth to truth, from lesser truth to higher truth—but it is never from error to truth. (II. 365)

Angels or gods, whatever you may call them, have all to become men, if they want to become perfect. (II. 271)

Man should not be degraded to worldly slavery but should be raised up to God. (II. 299)

There is no limit to man's power, the power of words and the power of mind. (I. 290)

The man who is pure and who dares, does all things. (VIII. 336)

The greater a man has become, the fiercer ordeal he has had to pass through. (VII. 126)

Know it for certain that there is no greater *Tirtha* (holy spot) than the body of man. (VII. 119-20)

Every man has his own burden to bear. (IV. 11)

The most practical man would call life neither good nor evil. (V. 240)

The highest man *cannot* work, for there is no binding element, no attachment, no ignorance in him. (V. 245)

Him I call a *Mahatma* (great soul) whose heart bleeds for the poor, otherwise he is a *Duratman* (wicked soul). (V. 58)

Instead of begging, the religious man should give. (VII. 417)

Men do not know what it is to love; if they did, they would not talk so glibly about it. (II. 47)

It is the men that make the country ! (V. 210)

*Men* are more valuable than all the wealth of the world. (V. 83)

*Men* we want, and how can men be made unless *Shraddha* is there? (V. 333)

A mass of reading does not make men; those who were real men were made so by personal contact. (V. 284)

Money and all will come of themselves, we want men, not money. (VI. 406)

In our country we at present need manhood and kindness. (VI. 410)

Mankind ought to be taught that religions are but the varied expressions of THE RELIGION, which is Oneness, so that each may choose that path that suits him best. (VI. 416)

There is hope for all. (II. 402)

Our only hope then lies in penetrating deeper. (II. 156)

## Manifestation

Perfection means infinity, and manifestation means limit,

and so it means that we shall become unlimited
limiteds, which is self-contradictory. (II. 172-73)
With manifestation comes limitation. (II. 460)
The difference is not in the soul but in the manifestation. (III. 126)

**Manifoldness**

Manifoldness is only apparent. (II. 192)
The manifold is not valueless. (VI. 51)
It is through the many that we reach the one. (VI. 51)

**Master**

Everyone can play the role of a master but it is very
difficult to be a servant. (VII. 447)
Only those who want nothing are masters of nature. (VII. 68)
Mastery elevates and servitude debases. (VII. 52)

**Material**

When the world is the end and God the means to attain
that end, that is material. (VI. 66)
Material science can only give worldly prosperity, whilst
spiritual science is for eternal life. (VI. 391)
Materialism and all its miseries can never be conquered
by materialism. (III. 277)

**Matter**

Matter is your servant, not you the servant of matter. (I. 11)
It is possible to demonstrate that what we call matter
does not exist at all. (II. 76)
Matter does not prove Spirit. (V. 54)

**Maya**

Maya, it is all Maya. (VI. 518)
Maya is a statement of the fact of this universe, of how it
is going on. (II. 94)

Maya cannot be said to exist. (II. 275)

This name and form is the outcome of what is called Maya. (II. 275)

Time, space and causation we call Maya. (VI. 93)

Space and time are in Maya. (II. 177)

Maya is neither existence nor non-existence. (VII. 99)

Maya is not real. (VIII. 247)

Maya is not illusion, as it is popularly interpreted. (VI. 92)

Maya is real, yet it is not real. (VI. 92)

Nature is Maya. (VIII. 247)

This mixture of life and death, good and evil, knowledge and ignorance is what is called Maya. (VI. 380)

All that binds us is Maya—delusion. (VIII. 22)

The substance is noumenon, Maya is pheno-menon. (VIII. 247)

The first is the question of creation, that this nature, Prakriti, Maya is infinite, without beginning. (III. 122)

In reality there is one, but in Maya it is appearing as many. (V. 309)

Maya means name and form, into which everything is cast. (VIII. 247)

All the differentiation in substance is made by name and form. (VIII. 247)

Our lives are but a passing from dream to dream. (VIII. 251)

It (Maya) is the screen that hides the Self, which is unchanging. (V. 284)

Everyone must sooner or later get rid of the bonds of Maya. (III. 445)

The children of Maya live for ever, but the children of enjoyment die. (III. 342)

We have to give up ignorance and all that is false, and then truth will begin to reveal itself to us. (II. 167)

Ignorance is the mother of all the evil and all the misery we see. (I. 53)

Ignorance is the cause of egoism, attachment, aversion, and clinging to life. (I. 237)

Seeing difference is the cause of all misery, and ignorance is the cause of seeing difference. (VII. 37)

One idea that I see clear as daylight is that misery is caused by ignorance and nothing else. (VII. 501)

There is no sin nor virtue, there is only ignorance. (V. 14-15)

Ignorance sees manifold. (IV. 233)

Ignorance is the cause of all this bondage. (III. 128)

The Omnipresent Lord has been hidden through ignorance, and the responsibility is on yourself. (III. 161)

It is ignorance that makes us hate each other, it is through ignorance that we do not know and do not love each other. (III. 241)

We all know we are, but not how we are. (VII. 34)

We do not know the world yet; it is only through freedom that we see what it is, and understand its nature. (II. 325)

Illusion always rests upon illusion; it never rests upon God, the Truth, the Atman. (II. 251)

This illusion of the universe will break one day. (III. 10)

Difference in identity means exclusion, and exclusion means limitation. (II. 460)

Coming and going is all pure delusion. (V. 68)

All pain of the Soul is simply delusion. (I. 237)

Delusion creates delusion. (VII. 65)

Delusion cannot touch the Atman. (VII. 65)

We are miserable through delusion. (II. 198)

Delusion cannot be called an existence. (III. 13)

It is delusion always that produces delusion. (III. 13)

Place, time, causation are all delusions. (VII. 73)

Deluded is he who happiness seeks. (IV. 495)

Heterogeneity is only in appearance. (VI. 125)

You are all mistaken in learning. (VI. 64)

It is a mistake to think that we are impure, that we are limited, that we are separate. (II. 280)

Life is nothing, death is nothing, hunger nothing, cold nothing. (V. 17)

All practice or worship is only for taking off this veil. (VI. 475)

It is the 'screen' that hides the Self which is unchanging. (VIII. 12)

Things are not what they seem. (VIII. 129)

## Meditation

The greatest help to spiritual life is meditation (*Dhyana*). (II. 37)

The greatest thing is meditation. (V. 253)

Meditation is the means of unification of the subject and object. (VI. 91)

Meditation means the mind is turned back upon itself. (IV. 235)

## Mercy

Mercy is heaven itself; to be good, we have all to be merciful. (I. 59)

# Mind

Mind and matter cannot explain each other. (IV. 380)

Mind becomes matter, and matter in its turn becomes mind. (VI. 34)

Matter at a high rate of vibration is what is known as mind. (VI. 34)

Mind at a very low rate of vibration is what is known as matter. (VI. 34)

Mind is material. (VI. 128)

Mind is very fine matter; it is the instrument for manifesting *Prana*. (VI. 128)

Mind is changed into matter, matter is changed into mind. (VIII. 246)

Both matter and mind exist in a third, a unity which divides itself into the two. (VII. 101)

It is the mind that makes the body. (V. 304)

Mind is the name of a stream of consciousness or thought continuously changing. (II. 272)

All difference is, therefore, due to the mind. (II. 461)

The mind is constantly changing and vacillating. (I. 135)

The whole world is in our own minds. (I. 441)

This unstable condition of the mind must be changed. (I. 426)

The binding link of 'I and Mine' is in the mind. (I. 101)

The powers of the mind are like rays of light dissipated; when they are concentrated, they illumine. (I. 129)

No two persons have the same mind or the same body. (I. 473-74)

The perfected mind can be attached to all the organs simultaneously. (I. 135)

If the mind is not under control, it is no use living in a
   cave because the same mind will bring all distur-
   bances there. (I. 440)

If the mind is under control, we can have the cave
   anywhere, wherever we are. (I. 440-411)

All minds are the same, different parts of one Mind. (II. 17)

All these extraordinary powers are in the mind of
   man. (II. 12)

All that we see, we project out of our own minds. (II. 49)

The mind will not receive new thoughts, because they
   bring discomfort. (II. 316)

This mind is like a lake, and every thought is like a wave
   upon that lake. (II. 268)

Each mind is connected with every other mind. (II. 13)

The mind is omnipresent and can be heard and felt
   anywhere. (VIII. 512)

The freedom of the mind is a delusion. (VI. 92)

The mind has to be killed. (VII. 195)

The body is here, beyond that is mind, yet the mind is
   not the Atman. (III. 126)

There is no desire for a peaceful mind. (V. 250)

Concentration of the mind is the source of all know-ledge.
   (VIII. 36)

It is our own mental attitude which makes the world what
   it is for us. (I. 441)

Time, space, and causation are the three conditions
   through which the mind perceives. (VI. 43)

Time, space and causation, therefore, are in the mind. (II. 78)

It is the cheerful mind that is persevering. (III. 69)

It is the strong mind that hews its way through a thousand
   difficulties. (III. 69)

The mind should always go towards God. (IV. 8)

The grosser the mind, the more difficult (it is) to control (it). (IV. 220)

The purer the mind, the easier it is to control it. (IV. 220)

When the mind becomes functionless, it reflects the Brahman-consciousness. (VI. 487)

The mind cannot reach the pure Self, no, nor even intellect. (VI. 475)

'Whys' and 'Wherefores' are in mind only. (VI. 44)

Mind-activity means creation. (VI. 100)

Our mind is acting on three planes: the subconscious, conscious, and superconscious. (VI. 128)

The mind uncontrolled and unguided will drag us down, down, for ever—rend us, kill us; and the mind controlled and guided will save us, free us. (VI. 30)

The direction of the mind, which always runs after the senses, has to be turned within. (VII. 195)

Anything, therefore, beyond mind must be beyond time, space, and causation. (VI. 43)

Always keep your mind joyful; if melancholy thoughts come, kick them out. (VI. 130)

The concentrated mind is a lamp that shows us every corner of the soul. (VII. 60)

What you have inside you is that you see in other. (VI. 129)

What we are, we see outside, for the world is our *mirror*. (VIII. 48)

He who has not darkness sees no darkness in others. (VI. 129)

Mental pains are more poignant than physical tortures. (V. 429)

Mental pleasures are greatly superior to physical joys.
(V. 429)

'Consciousness is a mere film between two oceans, the
sub-conscious and the superconscious.' (VIII. 276)

*Unchaste imagination is as bad as unchaste action.* (VII. 69)

Everyone's idea of pleasure is different. (II. 165)

He who has conquered the internal nature controls the
whole universe; it becomes his slave. (I. 257)

This has been the search (for the real) throughout the
history of the human mind. (II. 72)

## Misery

The misery that we suffer comes from ignorance, from
non-discrimination between the real and the
unreal. (I. 287)

All misery comes from fear, from unsatisfied desire. (I. 130)

The misery in the world is in the senses. (I. 515)

Misery is caused by sin, and by no other cause. (I. 265)

All the misery we have is of our own choosing. (I. 408)

We must be merciful towards those that are in misery.
(I. 222)

Misery comes because we think we are finite—we are
little beings. (II. 399)

There is no misery where there is no want. (II. 4)

All separations are misery. (IV. 249)

All the misery of the world is caused by the slavery to
the senses. (VI. 30)

Pain and misery are not in man. (VIII. 22)

## Money

Money does not pay, nor name; fame does not pay, nor
learning. (IV. 367)

Think not that you are poor; money is not power, but goodness, holiness. (V. 24)

Hold your money merely as custodian for what is God's. (VII. 61)

Money is not evil after all—in good hands. (VIII. 514)

## Monasticism

Real monasticism is not easy to attain. (VII. 251)

The monk is greater than the prince. (VIII. 89)

## Moral

Everything that strengthens the will by revealing the real nature is moral. (VIII. 225)

We are all brothers, and we shall be truly moral when we have realized religion. (II. 164)

Self-abnegation is the centre of all morality. (II. 83)

Morality is the path towards freedom, and immorality leads to bondage. (II. 141)

How can religion or morality begin without renunciation itself ? (III. 343)

The first requisite is to be moral. (IV. 220)

The foundation (must be) this perfect morality. (IV. 221)

Christ saw that the basis is not low, that morality and purity are the only strength. (V. 193)

Morality exists first; later religion codifies it. (VII. 58)

The watchword of all well-being, of all moral good is not 'I' but 'thou'. (II. 353)

## Mother

She it is whose shadow is life and death. (VI. 150)

She is the pleasure in all pleasures. (VI. 150)

She is the misery in all misery. (VI. 150)

We all think of ourselves, and never of the Mother. (VIII. 484)

Mother knows best, as I say always. (VIII. 494)

The position of the mother is the highest in the world. (I. 68)

Love Her because you are Her child. (VIII. 253)

See Her in all, good and bad alike. (VIII. 253)

Only resting in Mother are we safe. (VIII. 253)

The Mother is the ideal of love; she rules the family, she possesses the family. (VIII. 58)

We are putting on different garbs to help the Mother Spirit in Her play. (V. 254)

He—She—the Mother, is playing, and we are like dolls, Her helpers in this play. (V. 254)

Friends or foes, they are all instruments in Her hands to help us work out our own *Karma*, through pleasure or pain. (VI. 435)

The Mother is our guide and whatever happens or will happen is under Her ordination. (VI. 417)

Established in the idea of Mother, we can do anything. (VII. 27)

Every manifestation of power in the universe is 'Mother'. (VII. 26)

Behind every creature is the 'Mother', pure, lovely, never changing. (VII. 6)

Mother is the first manifestation of power and is considered a higher idea than father. (VII. 26)

Without propitiating the Mother by worship and obeisance, not even Brahma and Vishnu have the power to elude Her grasp and attain to freedom. (VII. 216)

The same sea in waves is Divine Mother. (VII. 27)

The Divine Mother is the *Kundalini* ('coiled up' power). (VII. 26)

The highest of all feminine types in India is mother, higher than wife. (VI. 149)

The one thing that fulfils womanhood, that is womanliness in woman, is motherhood. (VIII. 59)

To be brave is to have faith in the Mother. (VI. 149)

Love Her for Herself, without fear or favour. (VIII. 253)

Eternal, unquestioning self-surrender to Mother alone can give us peace. (VIII. 253)

May the Mother dance in your hearts and bring infinite strength to your arms. (VIII. 481)

May Mother enshrine Herself in your hearts as strength. (VIII. 433)

May She make you all fearless. (VIII. 433)

Mother (Holy Mother—Sarada Devi) has been born to revive that wonderful *Shakti* in India. (VII. 484)

The work of the Mother will not suffer; because it has been built and up to date maintained upon truth, sincerity, and purity. (V. 139)

**Motion**

Every motion is in a circle. (I. 196)

Motion is always a relative thing. (II. 79)

There is no motion in straight line. (II. 231)

Motion is the sign of life. (VIII. 325)

**Motto**

Sympathy for the poor, the downtrodden, even unto death—this is our motto. (V. 30)

**Music**

Music is the highest art and, to those who understand, is the highest worship. (V. 125)

**Mystic**

Mystics in every religion speak the same tongue and teach the same truth. (VI. 81)

**Mystery-Mongering**

Mystery-mongering weakens the human brain. (I. 134)

Mystery-mongering and superstition are always signs of weakness. (III. 279)

**Nation**

The more strength is infused into the national life, the more will language, art, and music, etc. become spontaneously instinct with ideas and life. (VI. 189)

Each nation has a mission for the world. (VIII. 75)

As soon as its mission is destroyed, the nation collapses. (VIII. 75)

Each nation must give in order to live. (III. 273)

Each nation has its own peculiar method of work. (III. 314)

Each nation has its own peculiarity and individuality with which it is born. (III. 148)

Each nation has a destiny to fulfil, each nation has a message to deliver, each nation has a mission to accomplish. (III. 369)

We cannot be twisted and tortured into the shape of other nations. (III. 219)

Giving up the senses makes a nation survive. (III. 205)

Each nation has a theme: everything else is secondary. (V. 210)

A nation is sure to die when the main purpose of its life is hurt. (V. 457)

A nation that has no history of its own has nothing in this world. (V. 365)

A nation is advanced in proportion as education and intelligence spread among the masses. (IV. 482)

In the well-being of one's own nation is one's own well-being. (IV. 472)

In each nation, as in music, there is a main note, a central theme, upon which all others turn. (V. 210)

Great enterprise, boundless courage, tremendous energy, and, above all, perfect obedience—these are the only traits that lead to individual and national regeneration. (VI. 349)

Bearing this in mind we shall be in a better position to understand why, for our national welfare, we must first seek out at the present day all the spiritual forces of the race, as was done in days of yore and will be done in all times to come. (III. 371)

## Nature

There is no progression or digression in nature. (VIII. 157)

Nature is homogenous. (VI. 34)

Nature is itself differentiation. (VI. 94)

Nature is name and form. (VIII. 247)

Nature also is nothing but a mass of contradictions. (VI. 117)

Nature is all this force, whether expressed as matter or mind. (VIII. 246)

Nature with its infinite power is only a machine; freedom alone constitutes sentient life. (V. 289)

Nature is but the mirror of our own selves. (VIII. 26)

Nature's justice is uniformly stern and unrelenting. (V. 240)

To give and take is the law of nature. (V. 356)

Nature grinds all of us. (IV. 247)

Nature has no light of its own. (I. 255)

Nature itself cannot destroy nature. (III. 161)

Man is not to regard *nature* as his goal, but something
     higher. (II. 64)

Our essential nature always remains the same. (II. 356)

Goodness is our nature, purity is our nature, and that
     nature can never be destroyed. (II. 356)

Good is our nature, perfection is our nature, not
     imperfection, not impurity. (III. 377)

There is no supernatural, says the Yogi, but there are in
     nature gross manifestations and subtle manifesta-
     tions. (I. 122)

In nature alone are forms. (I. 495)

All are helped on by nature. (I. 89)

The more you fly from nature, the more she follows you;
     and if you do not care for her at all, she becomes
     your slave. (I. 263)

Nature is like that screen which is hiding the reality
     beyond. (II. 82)

Uniformity is the rigorous law of nature; what once
     happened can happen always. (I. 127)

Nature never has power over you. (II. 128)

Nature is conquered by man everyday. (II. 465)

Nothing ever changes your nature, or ever will. (III. 9)

We are at the beck and call of nature. (IV. 247)

Every one acts according to his own nature. (VI. 48)

To worship is inherent in every man's nature; only the
     highest philosophy can rise to pure abstraction.
     (VIII. 33)

Man is born to conquer nature and not to follow it. (V. 409)

## Nirvana

*Nirvana* is the realization of the Self. (VIII. 12)

*Nirvana* can be attained here and now, that we do not
have to wait for death to reach it. (V. 284)

## Non-attachment

Why should we expect anything in return for what we
do ? (I. 77)

Without non-attachment there cannot be any kind of
yoga. (I. 101)

It is the theory of non-attachment, to be attached to
nothing while doing our work of life. (I. 87)

First, we have to attain this state of non-attachment and
then to work incessantly. (I. 101)

That is the secret; that non-attachment. (V. 254)

## Obedience

Everyone wants to command, and no one wants to
obey. (III. 134)

The first requisite for organization is obedience. (VI. 321)

The first thing needed is obedience. (VI. 322)

## Object

The object of life is to learn. (II. 502)

## Om

The manifesting word of God is *Om*. (I. 218)

*Om* represents the whole phenomena of sound-
producing. (I. 219)

*Om* has become the one symbol for the religious aspiration
of the vast majority of human beings. (I. 219)

His highest name is *Om*. (VII. 62)

To know the *Om* is to know the secret of the universe. (VIII. 3)

## Omnipresent

How can the omnipresent be born? (VI. 23)

## One

We pass from this valley of life and death to that One, where death and life do not exist, and we know the Real and become the Real. (V. 250)

The real is one. It is the mind which makes it appear as many. (V. 273)

Neither I nor thou nor you—It is all He the Lord, all One. (VI. 371)

The more a man advances towards oneness, the more ideas of 'I' and 'you' subside. (VI. 474)

## Opportunities

Opportunities will turn even a staunch moralist into a cheat. (VI. 349)

## Optimism

Not a work will be lost, no struggle vain, though hopes be blighted, powers gone. (IV. 390)

## Orient

The Orient has been the cradle of the human race for ages, and all the vicissitudes of fortune are there—kingdoms succeeding kingdoms, empires succeeding empires, human power, glory, and wealth, all rolling down there: a Golgotha of power and learning. (IV. 143-44)

## Overcautious

He who is overcautious about himself falls into dangers at every step. (VIII. 433)

## Pain

Pain has its uses. (III. 78)

## Patience

The seed grows into the tree, patiently and gently. (II. 117)

Patience, purity, and perseverance will prevail. (V. 62)

Patience is the best means of success. (VII. 445)

If you have infinite patience and perseverance, success is bound to come. (VI. 425)

It is the patient upbuilding of character, the intense struggle to *realize* the truth, which alone will tell in the future of humanity. (VIII. 335)

## Peace

What can be a greater giver of peace than renunciation? (IV. 404)

Flying from work is never the way to find peace. (IV. 130)

Blessed are the peacemakers, for they shall enjoy the earth. (VIII. 93)

## Perfection

Perfection is one thing and enjoyment another. (II. 161)

Perfection is always infinite. (II. 172)

Perfection means infinity. (II. 172)

Perfection is not to be attained, it is already within us. (II. 350)

Consciously or unconsciously, we are all striving for perfection. (I. 340)

Perfection comes through the disinterested performance of action. (IV. 137)

Perfection can never be attained by work. (V. 240)

Perfection is man's nature, only it is barred in and prevented from taking its proper course. (I. 292)

When a man is perfect he sees perfection in others. (III. 28)

Perfection does not come from belief or faith. (IV. 136-37)

Perfect life is a contradiction in terms. ... knowing this, we are bound to make the best of everything. (VI. 372)

In time, everyone will have perfect manifestation. (VI 456)

Perfection is already in man if he will see it. (VI. 354)

When a pitcher is being filled (by immersion), it gurgles, but when full, it is noiseless. (VI. 214)

## Perseverance

One must persevere, so that the grace may be received. (VI. 481)

Perseverance will finally conquer. (II. 152)

It is only those who persevere to the end that succeed. (V. 31)

Persons are but the embodiments, the illustrations of the principles. (III. 280)

## Philosophy

Poetry and philosophy will become friends. (II. 140)

Philosophy is the highest poetry. (VI. 63)

Philosophy is no joke or talk. (III. 10)

Our philosophy does not depend upon any personality for its truth. (V. 207)

**Physique**

First build up your physique. Then only you can get control over the mind. (VII. 155)

**Play**

It is all play. (II. 470)

It is all really in sport; the universe is His play going on. (III. 94)

We are all playing in this universe. (III. 94)

We are His chessmen; He puts the chessmen on the board and shakes them up. (III. 95)

**Pleasure**

Our pleasures are always changing. (II. 166)

**Poor**

The first of everything should go to the poor; we have only a right to what remains. (IV. 10)

**Poverty**

Poverty is not a synonym for holiness. (VIII. 226)

**Power**

It is the greatest manifestation of power to be calm. (I. 202)

Power is His and within His command. (I. 107)

The more power there is, the more bondage, the more fear. (VII. 64)

When thought is joined to will, we call it power. (VI. 129)

All want power, but few will wait to gain it for themselves. (VI. 136)

What we call powers, secrets of nature, and force, are all within. (I. 422)

Within you lies indomitable power. (VII. 144)

If one has got power, one must manifest it in action. (VI. 316)

The finer the instrument, the greater the power. (VI. 40)

Power is not the goal. (VI. 133)

Superhuman power is not strong enough. (II. 7)

There is no power in the universe to injure us unless we first injure ourselves. (III. 166)

Whenever power is used for evil, it becomes diabolical; it must be used for good only. (III. 298)

This is the one great idea to understand that our power is already ours, our salvation is already within us. (III. 410)

What we want is vigour in the blood, strength in the nerves, iron muscles and nerves of steel, not softening namby-pamby ideas. (III. 278)

What power is higher than the power of purity? (IV. 60)

Even the least work done for others awakens the power within. (V. 382)

Accumulation of power is as necessary as its diffusion. (IV. 458)

The same power is in everyone. (IV. 219)

There is no power on earth which can be kept long confined within a narrow limit. (IV. 141)

From the highest god to the meanest grass, the same power is present in all—whether manifested or not. (IV. 484)

## Practice

Practice is absolutely necessary. (I. 139)

It is practice first, and knowledge afterwards. (II. 317)

One ounce of practice is worth a thousand pounds of theory. (V. 304)

One ounce of the practice of righteousness and of spiritual Self-realization outweighs tons and tons of frothy talk and nonsensical sentiments. (III. 44)

The real work is in the practice. (III. 15)

External practices have value only as helps to develop internal purity. (III. 68)

Practice makes us what we shall be. (IV. 8)

## Prana

Everything is *Prana*; it is moving the sun, the moon, and the stars. (II. 30)

*Prana* is electricity, it is magnetism; it is thrown out by the brain as thought. (II. 30)

*Prana* is the driving power of the world, and can be seen in every manifestation of life. (VI. 128)

*Prana* is not breath, though it is usually so translated. It is the sum total of the cosmic energy. (I. 267)

The sum total of all forces in the universe, mental or physical, when resolved back to their original state, is called *Prana*. (I. 148)

*Pranayama* means the control of *Prana*. (I. 147)

From thought down to the lowest force, everything is but the manifestation of *Prana*. (I. 148)

## Prayer

Prayer and praise are the first means of growth. (VI. 90)

Prayer with the lips was not enough; people should pray with their hearts. (II. 493)

Better is silent prayer. (VIII. 102)

To pray for something is better than nothing. (VI. 68)

Be thou ever and ever my Love. (III. 99)

Pray, 'Thou our Father, our Mother, our dearest Friend ! Thou who bearest this universe, help us to bear the little burden of this our life.' (VI. 91)

Pray, 'I do not want wealth or beauty, this world or another, but Thee, O God ! Lord ! I have become weary. Oh, take me by the hand, Lord, I take shelter with Thee. Make me Thy servant. Be Thou my refuge.' (VI. 91)

Pray, 'Take us by the hand as a father takes his son, and leave us not.' (VI. 91)

Pray for knowledge and light, every other prayer is selfish. (I. 146)

Thou art my right, Thou my wrong, my Shiva. (VI. 303)

Open the gates of light, O Mother, to me Thy tired son. (VI. 176)

Rescue me, merciful Mother, from floating with desire. (VI. 176)

Thou art here, I see Thee. Thou art with me, I feel Thee. (VI. 262)

Thou Music of my Beloved's flute, lead on, I am following. (VI. 257)

When, When, O Lord, shall man be brother to man ? (V. 5)

May you be ever possessed of valour ! (VII. 504)

May the Lord ever protect you from illusion and delusion ! (VIII. 336)

Let us be good for our own sake on our own responsibility. (VIII. 279)

The giver of all gifts may give you all that is desirable on earth and in the end—which may He postpone to a day long, long ahead—may take you in His shelter of bliss and happiness and purity infinite. (VIII. 289)

May the blows you have received draw you closer to that Being who is the only one to be loved here and hereafter, so that you may realize Him in everything past, present, and future, and find everything present or lost in Him and Him alone. (VIII. 297)

Wilt Thou forsake me, Father of all good, Thou who knowest that *all* my life I am Thy servant and Thine alone? (VI. 304)

## Priestcraft

Priestcraft and tyranny go hand in hand. (III. 414)

## Principles

If the principles are there, the persons will come by the thousands and millions. (III. 280)

But principles are universal, *not* persons. (VI. 362)

Principles must conquer in the long run, for that is the manhood of man. (VI. 7)

## Privilege

The enjoyment of advantage over another is privilege. (I. 435)

The fight is to destroy that privilege. (I. 435)

## Progress

There is implanted in every man, naturally, a strong desire for progress. (IV. 456-57)

The test of progress is the amount of renunciation that one has attained. (VII. 211)

All real progress must be slow. (V. 193)

True progress is slow but sure. (V. 78)

All progression is in the relative world. (VII. 79)

## Prophet

Every prophet is a creation of his own times. (IV. 141)

The schools and colleges should be the training grounds for prophets. (VI. 10)

We have to work now so that everyone will become a
    prophet. (VI. 11)

Prophets are discoverers in the field of spirituality. (VI.9)

The whole universe must become prophets; and until a
    man becomes a prophet, religion is a mockery and a
    byword unto him. (VI. 10)

## Purity

In purity is no bondage. (VII. 103)

Perfect purity is the most essential thing, for only 'the
    pure in heart shall see God'. (VIII. 34)

*Out of purity and silence comes the word of power.* (VII. 16)

Purity in thought, speech, and act is absolutely necessary
    for anyone to be religious. (III. 48)

Perfect purity ensures the most lasting allegiance and
    confidence. (VI. 135)

To attain this purity of heart means long struggle and
    constant practice. (IV. 436)

Purity in every way is absolutely necessary. (IV. 24)

The power of purity; it is a definite power. (IV. 33)

That purity which is the goal of work is realizable only
    through doing good to others. (VI. 311)

Not to become pure, you are pure already. (II. 82)

If you are pure, you will reach God. (I. 413)

Only the pure in life can see God. (VIII. 47)

He reveals Himself to the pure heart; the pure and the
    stainless see God, yea, even in this life. (I. 13)

To gain this infinite universal individuality, this miserable
    little prison-individuality must go. (I. 14)

Work—this is the time; for the freshest, the untouched,
    and unsmelled flowers alone are to be laid at the
    feet of the Lord, and such He receives. (III. 304)

If you think yourself pure, pure you will be. (III. 130)

You must be pure and help anyone who comes to you, as much as lies in your power. (III. 142)

The purification of one's outer self is very necessary. (III. 361)

Spiritual truth is purity. (IV. 26)

Everything will come right if you are pure and sincere. (VI. 281)

If you are pure, if you are strong, *you, one man*, are equal to the whole world. (VI. 145)

Purity is strength. (IV. 133)

Purity of the mind must be insisted upon if you would control it. (VI. 126)

Purity of the mind is the first thing necessary. (V. 322)

The purer the body and mind, the quicker the desired result will be obtained. (VI. 125)

The purer the mind, the easier it is to control. (VI. 126)

Internal purity is of greater value than external. (I. 261)

Purity is the condition of His mercy. (I. 13)

The heart must be pure and the pure heart sees only good, never evil. (VIII. 20)

What is needed is *Chittashuddhi*, purification of the heart. (III. 301)

If we are pure, we cannot see impurity. (VII. 63)

Neither numbers nor powers nor wealth nor learning nor eloquence nor anything else will prevail, but *purity, living the life*, in one word, *Anubhuti*, realization. (VIII. 348)

Personal purity is imperative. (VI. 124)

Purity, patience, and perseverance are the three essentials to success and, above all, *love*. (VI. 281)

Purity, patience, and perseverance overcome all obstacles. (VI. 344)

There is nothing holier in the world than to keep good company, because the good impressions will then tend to come to the surface. (I. 220)

## Purusha

The Purusha is the only thing which is immaterial. (I. 135)

The Purusha is not the doer but the witness. (I. 361)

Love, existence, and knowledge are not the qualities of the Purusha, but its essence. (I. 249)

The Purusha does not love, it is love itself. (I. 249)

## Race

Each race has a peculiar mission to fulfil in the life of the world. (III. 108)

## Rajas

We want *Rajas* first, and *Sattva* will come afterwards—a thing far, far removed. (VII. 500)

## Ramakrishna

(The) books were theories, he (Ramakrishna) was the realization. (V. 53)

Shri Ramakrishna was both a *Jivanmukta* and an *Acharya*. (V. 269)

Shri Ramakrishna is a force. (V. 269)

He (Ramakrishna) is a power, living even now in his disciples and working in the world. (V. 269)

Never did come to this earth such an all-perfect man as Shri Ramakrishna. (VI. 480)

Ramakrishna Paramahamsa came for the good of the world. (VI. 266)

India can only rise by sitting at the feet of Shri Ramakrishna. (VI. 281)

It won't do merely to call Shri Ramakrishna an Incarnation, you must manifest power. (VI. 267)

Ramakrishna has no peer; nowhere else in this world exists that unprecedented perfection, that wonderful kindness for all that does not stop to justify itself, that intense sympathy for man in bondage. (VI. 231)

His life is the living commentary to the Vedas of all nations. (VI. 320)

What the whole Hindu race has thought in ages, he *lived* in one life. (VI. 320)

He who will bow before him will be converted into purest gold that very moment. (VI. 266)

From the day Shri Ramakrishna was born dates the growth of modern India and of the Golden Age. (VI. 318)

He was the living commentary to the Vedas and to their aim. (VII. 483)

His life is a searchlight of infinite power thrown upon the whole mass of Indian religious thought. (VII. 483)

Shri Ramakrishna was born to vivify all branches of art and culture in this country. (VII. 205)

In Shri Ramakrishna Paramahamsa the man was all dead and only God remained. (VII. 85)

Shri Ramakrishna's purity was that of a baby. (VII. 85)

He had lived in one life the whole cycle of the national religious existence in India. (VII. 483)

Ramakrishna Paramahamsa is the latest and the most perfect—the concentrated embodiment of knowledge, love, renunciation, catholicity, and the desire to serve mankind. (VII. 483)

Without studying Ramakrishna Paramahamsa first, one can never understand the real import of the Vedas, the Vedanta, of the Bhagavata and the other Puranas. (VII. 483)

One glance, one touch is enough. (VII. 8)

Ramakrishna had given us one great gift, the desire, and the lifelong struggle not to talk alone, but to *live the life*. (VIII. 348)

## Realization

Realization of love comes to none unless one becomes a perfect *Jnani*. (V. 385)

Realization is real religion, all the rest is only preparation. (I. 232)

Every moment of his life must be realization. (I. 111)

Religious realization does all the good to the world. (II. 286)

This realization alone is the soul of religion. (VI. 457)

It is this power of realization that makes religion. (V. 265)

The essential truth is realization. (VII. 211)

Not talking, theorising, argumentation but realization. (IV. 245)

What we experience in the depths of our souls is realization. (III. 54)

The only power is in realization, and that lies in ourselves and comes from thinking. (II. 336)

Realization will come in the fullness of time, by living constantly in the company of sadhus (holy men). (V. 268)

Realization is beyond virtue and vice, beyond future and past; beyond all the pairs of opposites. (VII. 70)

Hold we on to realization, to being Brahman, to becoming Brahman. (VIII. 349)

It was the same God, and the different realizations were only degrees and differences of vision. (VIII. 189)

Talking is one thing, and realizing is another. (II. 284)

This is to be seen, realized, not simply talked or thought about. (II. 318)

The man who realizes, 'I am He', though clad in rags, is happy. (VI. 82-83)

He who has realized the Atman becomes a storehouse of great power. (VII. 241)

Verification is the perfect proof of a theory. (I. 9)

We may talk and reason all our lives, but we shall not understand a word of truth, until we experience it ourselves. (I. 185)

It is not much use to talk about religion until one has felt it. (I. 127)

Until your religion makes you realize God, it is use-less. (I. 326)

If there is a God we must see Him, if there is a soul we must perceive it; otherwise it is better not to believe. (I. 127)

Nothing is easier to say, 'I work for work's sake', but nothing is so difficult to attain. (V. 241)

When a man realizes he gives up everything. (V. 309)

The first step upwards is when we recognize ourselves as the children of God; the last step is when we realize ourselves as the One, the Atman. (VIII. 16)

By thinking constantly of ghosts, men become ghosts themselves, while whoever repeats day and night, knowingly or unknowingly, 'I am the eternal, pure, free, self-illumined Atman', verily becomes the knower of Brahman. (VI. 518-19)

Forms vanish, rituals fly away, books are superseded; images, temples, churches, religions and sects, countries and nationalities—all these little limitations and bondages fall off by their own nature from him who knows this love of God. (III. 72)

If you know that you are positively other than your body, you have then none to fight with or struggle against; you are dead to all ideas of selfishness. (III. 84)

The kingdom of heaven is already in existence if we will have it, that perfection is already in man if he will see it. (VI. 354)

It is only when the sun is on our own head that *there is no shadow*. (VI. 379)

Light is everywhere visible only in the men of holiness. (VI. 118)

> I look behind and after
> And find that all is right.
> In my deepest sorrows
> There is a soul of light. (VI. 441)

## Reality

We must go to the Reality. (II. 174)

That reality we cannot see through the senses. (II. 156)

Our reality, therefore, consists in the Universal and not in the limited. (II. 79)

It is not an easy task to reach the state of seeing the Reality face to face. (VI. 115)

Real existence, real knowledge, and real love are eternally connected with one another, the three in one. (I. 58)

## Reason

We must reason. (VI. 13)

Reason helps inspiration. (VII. 41)

To reach truth by reason alone is impossible. (VI. 42)

Why was reason given us if we have to believe? (VI. 12)

Reason exists in nature; beyond nature it has no existence. (VI. 94)

Reason can go only to a certain extent, beyond that it cannot reach. (I. 150)

It is reason that develops into inspiration, and therefore inspiration does not contradict reason, but fulfils it. (II. 390)

It is better that mankind should become atheist by following reason than blindly believe in two hundred millions of gods on the authority of anybody. (II. 336)

Reasoning is the method of comparison between certain facts which we have already perceived. (II. 162)

Reason is the historian of the actions of the human being. (VII. 59)

Reasoning is limiting something by our own minds. (VII. 10)

We first perceive, then reason later. (VII. 75)

## Reform

Meddle not with so-called social reform, for there cannot be any reform without spiritual reform first. (V. 74)

## Relative

Life and death are but different names for the same fact, they are the two sides of one coin. (VIII. 30)

Life is ever expanding, contraction is death. (VI. 294)

Expansion is life, and contraction is death. (II. 500; IV. 366)

All expansion is life, all contraction is death. (VI. 320)

Life is the shadow of death, and death, the shadow of life. (V. 270)

Wherever there is life, with it there is death. (V. 270)

Love is life, and hatred is death. (IV. 366)

Life is nothing! Death is a delusion ! (V. 72)

It is life to do good, it is death not to do good to others. (IV. 367)

Where there is life, there will be death; so get away from life if you would be rid of death. (VI. 93)

Life and death are only different expressions of the same thing looked at from different standpoints. (I. 112)

Life and death are the same thing, looked at from different points. (I. 104)

We can never get rid of death until we get rid of life. (VI. 94)

Birth and death are in nature, not in you. (II. 278)

Birth and death belong to the body only. (V. 257)

Deny that there is any life at all, because life is only another name for death. (III. 17)

Life is one of these hallucinations, and death is its counterpart. (III. 17)

Then alone can death cease when I am one with life. (I. 14)

The only way to get beyond death is to give up the love of life. (I. 104)

Death I have conquered long ago when I gave up life. (VIII. 446)

Death is better than a vegetating ignorant life; it is better to die on the battle-field than to live a life of defeat. (II. 124)

It is better, far better, to die on the field of duty, preaching the truth, than to die like a worldly worm. (V. 114-15)

You live, because, millions die. (II. 112)

Ignorance is death, knowledge is life. (I. 52)

Good is life, evil is death. (VIII. 185)

Good and evil are inextricably combined, and one cannot be had without the other. (VII. 102)

There is no possibility of ever having pleasure without pain, good without evil; for living itself is just the lost equilibrium. (VII. 12)

You are born for good or evil. (VIII. 60)

Good and evil there always are in the world. (VIII. 110)

Good and evil have existence only in relation to us. (VIII. 22)

There is no good, and there is no evil. (VI. 53)

There are good and evil everywhere in this world. (VI. 54)

Good and evil are but superstitions, and do not exist. (II. 420)

That which is bad today may be good tomorrow. (I. 376-77)

That which is good today may be evil tomorrow. (I. 376)

There cannot be good without evil, nor evil without good. (I. 195)

Life is good or evil according to the state of mind in which we look at it, it is neither by itself. (I. 76)

Good and evil are the obverse and reverse of the same coin? (I. 84)

What is good for me may be bad for you. (I. 377)

Good action will entail upon us good effect; bad action, bad. (I. 53)

Wherever there is good, evil follows. (II. 181)

There is no such thing as absolute good, nor any such thing as absolute evil. (II. 165)

There is no such thing as good and bad. (II. 168)

As soon as we can give up good and evil it becomes a heaven. (II. 421)

Good and evil are not two things but one. (VI. 379)

To have good and no evil is childish nonsense. (VI. 380)

The sum total of good and evil in the world remains ever the same. (VI. 382)

Every bullet has its billet—evil goes with every good as its shadow. (VI. 379)

Only we have to learn that evil is destroyed by the growth of good. (V. 125)

Both *Pravritti* and *Nivritti* are of the nature of work: the former is evil work, and the latter is good work. (I. 86)

Evil and good are eternally conjoined, the obverse and the reverse of the same coin. (III. 214)

Independence is virtue; dependence is sin. (V. 419)

Faith in God and in one's own Self is virtue; doubt is sin. (V. 419)

Strength and manliness are virtue; weakness and cowardice are sin. (V. 419)

Knowledge of oneness is virtue; seeing diversity is sin. (V. 419)

Ignorance is the cause of which sin is the result. (VIII. 181)

We are to be saved from sin by being saved from ignorance. (VIII. 181)

That which tends to increase the divinity in you is virtue, and that which tends to increase brutality in you is vice. (VI. 112)

Eternal happiness and misery are a child's dream. (I. 452)

He who takes happiness, must take misery also. (I. 410)

Happiness and misery are the obverse and reverse of the same coin. (I. 409-10)

The only way of getting out of misery is by giving up the idea of happiness, because these two are linked to each other. (I. 104)

Misery is a greater teacher than happiness. (I. 27)

No more enjoyment; therefore no more misery. (III. 128)

All happiness which comes from the senses will, eventually, bring pain. (I. 243)

True happiness consists in killing selfishness. (I. 84)

All enjoyment will make us thirst for more, and that brings pain as its result. (I. 243)

All happiness is followed by misery as its shadow. (II. 177)

We get misery in return for our love. (II. 4)

After every happiness comes misery; they may be far apart or near. (VII. 11)

Attachment to the unreal will bring misery. (I. 442)

If you get attached, you become miserable. (I. 442)

So long as there is desire, no real happiness can come. (I. 186)

'The higher is your ideal, the more miserable you are'. (VIII. 389)

The more we think of ourselves as separate from the Whole, the more miserable we become. (II. 334)

Dualism is in nature, in manifestation, and monism is pure spirituality in the essence. (VI. 98)

Dualism is the natural idea of the senses. (III. 349)

The difference between dualism and monism is that when the ideal is put outside (of oneself), it is dualism. When God is (sought) within, it is monism. (II. 463)

Joy is one part of these hallucinations, and misery the other part. (III. 17)

So long as there are two, fear does not cease. (III. 417)

Wherever there is pleasure there must be pain. (VI. 93)

Pleasure and pain are meted out in equal measure. (II. 113)

With pleasure there is pain, and with pain, pleasure. (I. 410)

There is a pleasure in suffering even, when it is for others. (VIII. 484)

We are never attached where we do not find pleasure. (I. 239)

Wherever we find pleasure, there we are attached. (I. 239)

The cause is always known in and through the effect. (VI. 55)

Wheresoever there is a cause, there an effect must be produced. (I. 94)

The cause must have its effect; nothing can prevent or restrain this. (I. 82)

The effect is the cause in another form. (I. 417)

Where no bondage is, there is no cause and effect. (VII. 103)

(And just) as it is here in microcosm, it is exactly the same in the macrocosm. (II. 16)

The microcosm is but a miniature repetition of the macrocosm. (IV. 181)

The microcosm and the macrocosm are built on exactly the same plan. (II. 449)

The knowledge of the microcosm must lead to the knowledge of the macrocosm. (III. 56)

What is not here cannot be there. (I. 355)

The universe is you yourself. (II. 462)

We cannot see outside what we are not inside. (VII. 28)

What is within is without. (II. 327)

What is anywhere must be everywhere. (IV. 215)

Darkness and light always go together. (IV. 454)

Darkness is less light; evil is less good; impurity is less purity. (II. 327)

Impersonality includes all personalities. (II. 319)

The Impersonal includes the Personal. (II. 323)

The ignorant see the person in the non-person. The sage sees the non-person in the person. (VIII. 429)

You cannot serve God and Mammon at the same time. (VIII. 213)

Everybody should know that there is no salvation except through the conquering of desires. (III. 139)

Day and night never come together; so desire and the Lord can never come together. (VII. 91)

The more we go away, the more God comes in. (VII. 14)

As you are, He is. (VIII. 256)

The wicked see in God wickedness, the virtuous see in Him virtue. (VI. 116-17)

If you think you are bound, bound you will remain; if you know that you are free, free you are. (I. 419)

From freedom it comes, in bondage it rests, and goes back into that freedom again. (I. 96)

All idea of separation is bondage, that of non-differentiation is *Mukti*. (VI. 410-11)

Wherever there is thought, there must be words. (I. 397)

Ideas and words are in their nature inseparable. (I. 73)

Thought can only manifest itself through word. (I. 448)

There cannot be any thought without the word. (I. 448)

Where is no thought, there will be no work. (II. 86)

Thought and word are inseparable. (III. 57)

There cannot come the idea of form without the idea of name. (II. 42)

Whatever we do reacts upon us. (I. 397)

It is better to do something than to stand still. (I. 440)

What we have done, that we can undo. (I. 320)

Our actions do not harmonize with our thoughts. (I. 458)

There is one thing which is the world and another which is God; and this distinction is very true. (I. 87)

The difference between God and the devil is in nothing except in unselfishness and selfishness. (I. 425)

Unity is knowledge, diversity is ignorance. (VIII. 138)

Whenever mankind attains a higher vision, the lower vision disappears of itself. (VIII. 346)

The more our bliss is within, the more spiritual we are. (VIII. 29)

The more the shades around deepen, the more the ends approach and the more one understands the true meaning of life, that it is a dream. (VIII. 344)

The more we sink the 'little self', the more God comes. (VIII. 31)

More of goodness, less of artificial laws. (VI. 100)

The more selfish a man, the more immoral he is. (II. 352)

The more we know the better for us. (II. 355)

The more heart you will be able to manifest, the greater will be the victory you achieve. (VI. 425)

The more perfect, the less imperfections you see. (VIII. 234)

The less passion there is, the better we work. (II. 293)

Descent is very bad, and the ascent is the worst part

of the job, that's the same in everything in the world. (VIII. 323)

When the reflector is base, the reflection is bad. (VIII. 180)

Because it (the Self) cannot die, it cannot live. (V. 256)

Where it begins, there it ends. (V. 256)

To every action, there is equal reaction. (IV. 229)

If you want the reward, you must also have the punishment. (I. 104)

'Hard as steel and soft as a flower' is the motto. (VIII. 434)

The child is the man involved and the man is the child evolved. (II. 228)

None else has the blame, none has the praise. (II. 224)

The cause of the unconscious is the conscious. (II. 35)

The only way to get out of the punishment is to give up the reward. (I. 104)

No error can lead to truth. (I. 385)

If the world is created for us, we are also created for the world. (I. 88)

Change the subject, and the object is bound to change. (I. 426)

The weaker the man, the less he has of restraint. (I. 206)

Without chastity, there can be no spiritual strength. (I. 263)

Whatever ceases to expand, ceases to live. (II. 500)

If there is no desire, there is no suffering. (II. 147)

So long as there is desire or want, it is a sure sign that there is imperfection. (II. 261)

He who chooses perfection becomes pure. (II. 161)

He who chooses enjoyment misses his true end. (II. 161)

The gross can be easily perceived by the senses; not so the subtle. (I. 122)

It is better to be an outspoken atheist than a hypocrite. (I. 127)

The bound can only be explained by the free, the caused by the uncaused. (IV. 255)

It is only when the need is there that the demand will come. (IV. 19)

It is better to wear out than rust out. (VI. 406)

There is more difference between minds than between bodies. (VI. 109)

The mind acts on the body, and the body in its turn acts upon the mind. (VI. 39)

It takes a long time to earn but a short time to distri-bute. (VI. 136)

Atheists and materialists can have ethics, but only believers in the Lord can have religion. (VII. 80-81)

Every desire is fraught with evil, whether the desire itself be good or evil. (VII. 66)

Either *Bhoga* or Yoga—either enjoy this life, or give up and be a Yogi; *none can have both in one*. (VIII. 391)

Nature is one thing, soul another, eternally separate. (I. 253)

The church goes from the outside in; the mystic goes from the inside out. (VI. 81)

If we can bring ourselves down by our *Karma*, surely it is in our power to raise ourselves by it. (V. 213-14)

We learn, through smiles and tears we learn. (VIII. 493)

Absence of the thought of self is the essential characteristic of the love for God. (VIII. 203)

It is not the receiver that is blessed, but it is the giver. (I. 76)

Harmony and Peace and not Dissension. (I. 24)

We have either to go forward or to go backward. (III. 195)

We have either to progress or to degenerate. (III. 195)

When you see illusion, you do not see reality. (III. 21)

The first step to deserve is to desire. (IV. 301)

The voice of Asia has been the voice of religion. The voice of Europe is the voice of politics. (IV. 142)

Every improvement is coupled with an equal degradation. (VI. 379)

This ebb and flow, this rising and falling, is in the world's very nature. (I. 112)

Hinduism cannot live without Buddhism, nor Buddhism without Hinduism. (I. 23)

If matter is powerful, thought is omnipotent. (II. 302)

This present, this expressed, is only one part of that unexpressed. (III. 2)

You are a machine for taking and giving: you take, in order to give. (II. 5)

It is very easy to break down. ...but it would be hard for him to build up anything. (II. 116)

The more you struggle, the more enveloped you become. (IV. 39)

It is good and very grand to conquer external nature, but grander still to conquer our internal nature. (II. 65)

It is grand and good to know the laws that govern the stars and planets; it is infinitely grander and better to know the laws that govern the passions, the feelings, the will, of mankind. (II. 65)

From perfect knowledge, true love is inseparable. (III. 34)

It is from the finer that the grosser has come. (III. 400)

There cannot be friendship without equality. (III. 318)

Poverty there must be, so long as the disease known as civilization existed: and hence the need for relief. (III. 305)

Negation implies affirmation of the Real Self. (V. 283)

Light and darkness cannot remain together. (VI. 119)

## Religion

Religion alone is all that we have and mean to have. (III. 137)

Talking is not religion; parrots may talk, machines may talk nowadays. (III. 134)

Religion is to be realized, not only heard; It Is not in learning some doctrine like a parrot. (III. 378)

Ours is the only true religion because, according to it, this little sense-world of three day's duration is not to be made the end and aim of all, is not to be our great goal. (III. 180)

Our religion is not based upon persons but on principles. (III. 249)

Ours is the only religion that does not depend on a person or persons; it is based upon principles. (III. 280)

All religion is to be based upon morality, and personal purity is to be counted superior to *Dharma*. (III. 360)

Religion is not going to church, or putting marks on the forehead; or dressing in a peculiar fashion. (III. 283)

Religion is primary. (III. 289)

Religion is infinite, none can go beyond it. (III. 245)

Religion is not in books, nor in theories, nor in dogmas, nor in talking, not even in reasoning. It is being and becoming. (III. 253)

Religion belongs to the supersensuous and not to the sense plane. (III. 1)

Religions do not come from without but from within. (III. 1)

Religion does not live on bread, does not dwell in a house. (III. 3)

One religion cannot suit all. (III. 359)

That is religion which makes us realize the Unchangeable One, and that is the religion for everyone. (III. 283)

Religion, which is the highest knowledge and the highest wisdom, cannot be bought, nor can it be acquired from books. (III. 52)

It is an insult to a starving people to offer them religion; it is an insult to a starving man to teach him metaphysics. (I. 20)

Give up ! That is the watch-word of the Indian religions. (III. 148)

Temples or churches, books or forms, are simply the kindergarten of religion. (II. 43)

Science and religion will meet and shake hands. (II. 140)

Religion is ever a practical science, and there never was nor will be any theological religion. (II. 317)

Religion can be realized. (II. 285)

Realization is the soul, the very essence of religion. (II. 285)

Religion is not in doctrines, in dogmas, nor in intellectual argumentation; it is being and becoming, it is realization. (II. 43)

If a religion cannot help man wherever he may be, wherever he stands, it is not of much use. (II. 300)

The proof of one religion depends on the proof of the rest. (I. 318)

The first sign that you are becoming religious is that you are becoming cheerful. (I. 264)

The goal of all religions is the same, but the language of the teachers differs. (I. 342)

The proof of religion depends on the truth of the constitution of man, and not on any books. (I. 369)

The end of all religions is the realizing of God in the soul. (I. 324)

The man who is frightened into religion has no religion at all. (I. 327)

There is one religion and there are many sects. (I. 438)

There never were two religions. (I. 438)

The greatest religion is to be true to your own nature. (I. 483)

Books never make religions but religions make books. (I. 324)

Every religion is only evolving a God out of the material man, and the same God is the inspirer of all of them. (I. 18)

True religion is entirely transcendental. (I. 416)

Religion is not an imitation of Jesus or Mohammad. (I. 483)

No man can be religious until he has the same perceptions himself. (I. 127)

No two persons have the same religion. (I. 474)

Real religion begins where this little universe ends. (I. 97)

Religion is a constitutional necessity of the human mind. (I. 318)

Religion cannot be swallowed in the form of a pill. (I. 407)

Religion believes that there has been, and still is, one religion in the world. (I. 438)

Religion means realization, nothing else. (I. 468)

Religion is the realization of spirit as spirit. (I. 469)

Intellectual assent and intellectual dissent are not religion. (I. 232)

Religion is a question of fact, not of talk. (II. 163)

Religion comes when that actual realization in our own souls begins. (II. 164)

Religion is to us a mere intellectual assent, a mere talk, a mere nothing. (II. 164)

Religion is the search after the highest ideal. (II. 463)

Religion is the manifestation of the soul nature. (II. 478)

Beliefs, doctrines, sermons do not make religion. (II. 474)

Religion is realization; not talk, nor doctrine, nor theories, however beautiful they may be. (II. 396)

Religion is the highest plane of human thought and life. (II. 375)

1 shall call you religious from the day you begin to see God in men and women. (II. 326)

Religion as a science, as a study, is the greatest and healthiest exercise that the human mind can have. (II. 66)

Religion is the greatest motive power for realizing that infinite energy which is the birthright and nature of every man. (II. 67)

Religion is the highest motive power. (II. 67)

The religious ideals of the future must embrace all that exists in the world. (II. 67)

Religions must also be inclusive. (II. 67)

Therefore, religions will have to broaden. (II. 68)

Religious ideas will have to become universal, vast, and infinite. (II. 68)

Religion begins with this question (Is this real?) and ends with its answer. (II. 70)

All narrow, limited, fighting ideas of religion have to go. (II. 67)

Every religion insists on our having faith. (II. 162)

Each religion is living. (II. 366)

Only the man who has actually perceived God and soul has religion. (II. 163)

When we come to the real, spiritual, universal concept, then, and then alone, religion will become real and living. (II. 68)

What is needed is a fellow-feeling between the different types of religion. (II. 68)

No impure soul can be really religious. (III. 48)

There is no mystery in religion. (III. 278)

This is religion—renunciation. (III. 70)

It is a man-making religion that we want. (III. 224)

The fear of God is the beginning of religion, but the love of God is the end of religion. (VI. 71)

The goal of every religion is the same. (IV. 174)

Practical religion is identifying myself with my Self. (IV. 244)

One infinite religion existed all through eternity and will ever exist, and this religion is expressing itself in various countries in various ways. (IV. 180)

Religion wants to know the truth. (IV. 208)

True religion is positive and not negative. (IV. 190)

It is the power of realization that makes religion. (IV. 35)

No one who is the least impure will ever become religious. (IV. 58)

Religion is its own end. (IV. 279)

Religion is the manifestation of the Divinity already in man. (IV. 358)

To realize the spirit as spirit is practical religion. (IV. 247)

Religion is realization, and you must make the sharpest distinction between talk and realization. (IV. 30)

Religion is a long, slow process. (IV. 36)

Religion is neither talk, nor theory, nor intellectual consent. (IV. 125)

Religion permeates the whole of man's life, not only the present but the past, present, and future. (IV. 209; III. 4)

Religion does not consist in believing any number of doctrines or dogmas, in going to churches or temples, in reading certain books. (IV. 215)

Religion is a question of being and becoming, not of believing. (IV. 216)

Religion is the tie, unity of humanity. (IV. 143)

Religion is not talk, or doctrines, or theories; nor is it sectarianism. (IV. 179)

'Religion can be given and taken more tangibly, more really than anything else in the world.' (IV. 179)

Religion cannot live in sects and societies. (IV. 179)

Religion does not consist in erecting temples, or building churches, or attending public worship. (IV. 179)

Religion is realization. (IV. 182)

Religion consists in realization. (IV. 180)

At the core, all sects and all religions have the same aim. (IV. 174)

They (all religions) are the radii of the same truth, the expression that variety of minds requires. (V. 191)

Religion is of deeper importance than politics, since it goes to the root, and deals with the essential of conduct. (V. 200)

No one is born into a religion, but each one is born for a religion. (V. 411)

All religions are different expressions of the same truth. (V. 191)

The Hindu religion never persecutes. (V. 190)

Religion is not in fault. (V. 14)

Religion is not a thing of imagination but of direct perception. (V. 414)

Religion is the realizing of God. (V. 417)

Religion is realizing, and I shall call you a worshipper of God when you have become able to realize the Idea. (V. 265)

Religion goes to the root of the matter. If it is right, all is right. (V. 202)

The essence of all religions is the annihilation of desire. (V. 147)

Religion is the realization of Spirit as Spirit; not Spirit as matter. (VI. 98)

The book from which to learn religion is your own mind and heart. (VI. 81)

Religion has nothing to do with the senses. (VI. 132)

Religion is not, and never can be, in the field of intellect. (VI. 132)

No man is born to any religion; he has a religion in his own soul. (VI. 82)

We must see religion, feel it, realize it in a thousand times more intense a sense than that in which we see the wall. (VI. 10)

Learning has no place in religion; for the majority learning is a block in the way. (VI. 64)

Know that service to these (poor, illiterate, ignorant, and afflicted) alone is the highest religion. (VI. 288)

No one form of religion will do for all. (VI. 82)

When principles are entirely lost sight of and emotions prevail, religions degenerate into fanaticism and sectarianism. (VI. 8)

The whole of religion is our own inner perception. (VI. 64)

The end and aim of all religions is to realize God. (VI. 82)

Every religion is an expression, a language to express the same truth, and we must speak to each in his own language. (VI. 331)

Doing good to others is the one great universal religion. (VI. 403)

Altruistic service only is religion. (VI. 395)

All religions are true. (VI. 117)

All religions are divided into theory and practice. (VI. 41)

Religion is one, but its application must be various. (VI. 82)

Religion is of the soul and finds expression through various nations, languages, and customs. (VI. 46)

Religion is fundamental in the very soul of humanity. (VI. 46)

The religion of the Vedas is the religion of the Hindus, and the foundation of all Oriental religions. (VI. 48)

The evils exist not with, but against, religion. Religion therefore is not to blame, but men. (VI. 255)

Religion is to be realized now. (VI. 13)

Religion comes with intense self-sacrifice. (VI. 83)

The secret of religion lies not in theories but in practice. (VI. 245)

Religion is a growth. (VI. 98)

The idol is the expression of religion. (VI. 115)

Verification is the only proof of religious truth. (VII. 9)

Religion is not the outcome of the weakness of human nature; religion is not here because we fear a tyrant; religion is love, unfolding, expanding, growing. (VII. 421)

Religion is not in sects, nor in making a fuss—why do you forget these teachings of our revered Master? (VII. 446)

Intellect ends where religion begins. (VII. 91)

Religion begins where philosophy ends. (VII. 44)

Religion gives you nothing new; it only takes off obstacles and lets you see your Self. (VII. 62)

Religion is above reason, supernatural. (VII. 60)

Religion consists solely in realization. (VII. 96)

Talking, talking religion is but little good. (VII. 77)

Religious teaching must always be constructive, not destructive. (VII. 98)

Religion is philosophy concretized through rituals and symbols. (VIII. 356)

All the religions are good, since the essentials are the same. (VIII. 218)

Religion was never preached by planners ! (VIII. 261)

The two great watchwords of every great religion are renunciation and self-sacrifice. (VIII. 239)

The old religion can only be revivified by a new centre. (VIII. 308)

Every new religious wave requires a new centre. (VIII. 308)

Religion is the manifestation of the natural strength that is in man. (VIII. 185)

Religion does not depend upon knowledge. (VIII. 210)

All the various practices and trainings, Bibles and Gods, are but the rudiments of religion, the kindergartens of religion. (VIII. 140)

Throughout all religious systems and ideals is the same morality. (VIII. 138)

Religion is that which does not depend upon books or teachers or prophets or saviours, and that which does not make us dependent in this or in any other lives upon others. (VIII. 523)

If there were not different religions, no religion would survive. (VIII. 217)

In religion there must be *growth*. (VIII. 220)

All religions lead to God. (VIII. 24)

We must be bright and cheerful, long faces do not make religion. (VIII. 7)

Religion should be the most joyful thing in the world, because it is the best. (VIII. 7)

The essential thing in religion is making the heart pure; the Kingdom of Heaven is within us, but only the pure in heart can see the King. (VIII. 8)

Religion is the science which learns the transcendental in nature through the transcendental in man. (VIII. 20-21)

The one great secret of religion is to know for yourself that you are a spirit. (VIII. 234)

Religion lives inside. (VIII. 233)

Religion is experience. (VIII. 230)

Religion is not intellectual jargon at all, but realization. (VIII. 230)

Religion lies in being and becoming, in realization. (VIII. 229)

Religious truths need verification by everyone. (VI. 133)

Religious quarrels are always over the husks. (VI. 127)

Real religion is one; all quarrel is with the forms, the symbols, the 'illustrations'. (VIII. 33)

All religions and all methods of work and worship lead us to one and the same goal. (I. 108)

All the religions, from the lowest fetishism to the highest absolutism, mean so many attempts of the human soul to grasp and realize the Infinite. (I. 17)

If one religion is true, all the others must be true. (I. 318)

In essentials, all religions are one. (I. 318)

It is the same religion (presenting) different aspects in different places. (I. 438)

When a man is gloomy, that may be dyspepsia, but it is not religion. (I. 264)

No religion, built upon a person, can be taken up as a type by all the races of mankind. (III. 250)

Until you have that thirst, that desire, you cannot get religion. (II. 45)

Wherever there are business and business principles in religion, spirituality dies. (IV. 179)

Impart even secular knowledge through religion. (V. 213)

There is no greater *Dharma* than this service of living beings. (VI. 502)

It is in love that religion exists and not in ceremony. (III. 141)

Religion does not consist in talk, or doctrines, or books, but in realization; it is not learning, but *being*. (IV. 35)

It is religion, the inquiry into the beyond, that makes the difference between man and an animal. (III. 3)

It is very good to be born in a church, but it is very bad to die in a church. (II. 39)

It is good, to be born in a temple, but woe unto the person who dies in a temple or church. (II. 474)

## Remembrance

*Remembering* is as good as *seeing*. (III. 35)

He who is near can be seen, but he who is far can only be remembered. (III. 34-35)

## Remedy

The only remedy is in making unselfish men and women. (II. 495)

## Renunciation

This is the one great duty, this is renunciation. (II. 37)

Renunciation is the very basis upon which ethics stands. (II. 62)

Renunciation is the very basis of our true life. (II. 174)

The ideal of renunciation nowhere attains such a height as in the teachings of the Vedanta. (II. 146)

This is the stepping-stone and the real centre and the real heart of all spiritual culture—renunciation. (III.70)

This is the land of renunciation. (III. 353)

The grand lesson we shall ever teach to humanity will be renunciation. (III. 354)

The Alpha and Omega is renunciation. (III. 343)

Through renunciation alone this immortality is to be reached. (III. 343)

Through renunciation is the way to the goal and not through enjoyment. (III. 180)

There is no end to renunciation. (IV. 243)

Our solution is unworldliness—renunciation. (IV. 315)

Renunciation is the background of all religious thought wherever it be. (IV. 183)

Renunciation, and renunciation alone, is the real secret, the *Mulamantra*, of all Realization. (V. 397)

The essential thing is renunciation. (V. 382)

Renunciation is the evolution of nature and the manifestation of the God within. (V. 281)

To live in the world and not to be of it is the true test of renunciation. (V. 272)

Renunciation is the very soul of the Upanishads. (VI. 507)

There is no way, none whatsoever, to the solution of the profound mystery of this life except through renunciation. (VI. 488)

Renunciation must come but in the fullness of time. (VII. 240)

Renunciation is not asceticism. (VIII. 226)

Everything is fraught with fear : Renunciation alone is fearless. (VIII. 279)

Renunciation is in our blood. (VIII. 406)

It is renunciation, *tyaga*, that is meant by religion, and nothing else. (VIII. 385)

Renunciation means that none can serve both God and Mammon. (VIII. 223)

There is nothing so high as renunciation of self. (V. 78)

Renunciation is always the ideal of every race. (VIII. 524)

Without enjoyment, renunciation can never come. (V. 447)

First enjoy and then you can renounce. (V. 447)

Renunciation is the word—'नान्यः पन्था विद्यते अयनाय—There is no other way than this.' (VI. 505)

Renunciation is of the mind. (VIII. 226)

When he has controlled the senses, he has renounced. (VIII. 227)

If you desire to attain God, you will have to renounce *Kama-Kanchana* (lust and possession). (III. 451)

There will be no spiritual strength unless one renounces the world. (VI. 276)

The renunciation of *Kama-Kanchana* is the most important. (V. 261)

If you can give up, you will have religion. (III. 343)

We are here to know truth, not for enjoyment. (VIII. 37)

We love not for the long purse, we never sell our love, we want not, we give. (VI. 258)

Self-love is the first teacher of self-renunciation. (IV. 471)

## Resolution

We must have faith in ourselves; we must become world-movers, for everything is in us. (III. 175)

Hundreds will fall in the struggle, hundreds will be ready to take it up. (V. 17)

Wish is half the work. (VIII. 487)

Each one will have to save himself, each one to do his own work. (VII. 487)

None of us can get anything other than what we fix our hearts upon. (III. 48)

## Reverence

Reverence is a growth out of love; we can none of us revere him whom we do not love. (III. 79)

## Rishis

Rishis were spiritual discoverers. (III. 119)

Great Rishis will appear and lead us to customs and manners that are suited to new environments. (III. 112)

The Rishi as he is called in the Upanishads is not an ordinary man, but a *Mantra-drashta*. (III. 175)

The term Rishi means 'the seer of the truth of the *Mantras*', and not any Brahmin with the holy thread hanging down the neck. (VI. 496)

## Rituals

Rituals are the kindergarten of religion. (V. 216)

Old rituals must be rejected and new ones substituted. (V. 217)

Ritual is in fact concretized philosophy. (I. 72)

## Ruler

He is the best ruler who can serve well. (V. 61)

## Sacrifice

No great work can be done without sacrifice. (IV. 352)

No great work has been done in the world without sacrifice. (VIII. 216)

Great things can be done by great sacrifices only. (V. 34)

Nothing is gained except by sacrifice. (I. 520)

Sacrifice in the past has been the Law, it will be, alas, for ages to come. (VII. 501)

The martial spirit is not self-assertion but self-sacrifice. (VII. 270)

## Sadhana

We have to cover everything with the Lord Himself. (II. 146)

Bodilessness must be the ideal. (II. 350)

We have to go beyond the body, and beyond thought too. (II. 350)

Nothing can be done in a day. (II. 152)

Voluntarily weakening the body is really no prescription for spiritual enlightenment. (III. 69)

Great convictions are the mothers of great deeds. (V. 30)

Those that persevere will see the light, sooner or later. (V. 104)

Doing good to others constitutes a way, a means of revealing one's own Self or Atman. (VII. 112)

To control our passions we have to control them at their very roots; then alone shall we be able to burn out their very seeds. (I. 242)

All that man has to do is to take care of three things; good thought, good word, good deed. (I. 492)

Unhealthy persons cannot be Yogis. (I. 221)

The negative way is the most difficult. (I. 98)

The early morning and the early evening are the two periods of calmness. (I. 145)

And, above all, if the pride of spirituality enters into you, woe unto you. (I. 429)

Miracles are only stumbling-blocks. (I. 328)

Those that only take a nibble here and a nibble there will never attain anything. (I. 177)

Nothing is done in a day. (I. 407)

The only way to come out of bondage is to go beyond the limitations of law, to go beyond causation. (I. 98)

We can use one thorn to extract another and then throw both away. (III. 17)

The way is very difficult, like walking on the edge of a razor. (II. 124)

This, O Nachiketas, is very difficult, the way is long, and it is hard to attain. (II. 410)

Hiding facts is not the way to find a remedy. (II. 94)

Nobody ever got anything by begging. (IV. 301)

Don't-touchism is a form of mental disease. (VI. 320)

Until that thirst is awakened in you, you are no better than any atheist. (II. 45)

Taking a step backward, you do not avoid any misfortune. (I. 461)

My way is good for me, but not for you. (III. 131)

Restraint does not come in one day, but by long continued practice. (I. 208)

Very few have the power to grasp the higher, fewer still the patience to attain to it. (I. 142)

## Salvation

Salvation never will come through hope of reward. (II. 243)

What is salvation? To live with God. (III. 537)

There is no salvation for man until he sees God, realizes his own soul. (III. 378)

Our salvation is already within us. (III. 410)

To be unselfish, perfectly selfless, is salvation itself; for the man within dies, and God alone remains. (IV. 150)

There is salvation only for the brave. (I. 479)

Salvation means knowing the truth. (I. 512)

The road to salvation is through truth. (I. 499)

Salvation (comes) by faith and not by work. (I. 512)

*Mukti* means entire freedom—freedom from the bondages of good and evil. (V. 317)

There is no *Mukti* on earth to call my own. (VI. 266)

To get out of this infinite chain of causation is *Mukti* (freedom). (VI. 118)

## Samadhi

*Samadhi* is the means through which we can gain anything and everything, mental, moral, or spiritual. (I. 291)

## Samsara

It is *Samsara*, continuous motion; it is *Jagat*. (III. 416)

The *Samsara* is unreal, hollow, void of substance. Unless you give it up, you can never reach God, try however you may. (III. 451)

It is all misery, this *Samsara*. (V. 112)

## Sannyasa

Sacrifice of everything for the good of others is real. (VII. 245)

## Sannyasin

A Sannyasin cannot belong to any religion. (V. 260)

The Sannyasin is to love death. (III. 446)

## Sanskrit

Sanskrit is the language of God. (III. 513)

Sanskrit is the divine language. (III. 513)

Sanskrit and prestige go together in India. (III. 299)

The very sound of Sanskrit words gives a prestige and a power and a strength to the race. (III. 290)

## Sattva

*Sattva* is nearly *Nitya*. (IV. 405)

What can bring greater strength than *Sattvaguna* (absolute purity of mind) ? (IV. 404)

With *Sattva* only, comes wisdom. (VII. 39)

## Science

Each science must have its own methods. (I. 128)

Science is nothing but the finding of unity. (I. 14)

## Scripture

In no other scripture in the world is this adjective (fearless) applied either to God or to man. *Abhih*, fearless ! (III. 237)

No scriptures can make us religious. (I. 412)

## Self

You are the Self, and that must be realized. (IV. 245)

No food or drink can taint that noble Self which knows Itself. (IV. 395)

I worship my Self. (II. 472)

There is really but one Self in the universe, all else is but Its manifestations. (V. 411)

Your religion teaches you that every being is only your own self multiplied. (V. 14)

We are the Self, eternally at rest and at peace. (V. 274)

There is nothing so certain in me as my Self. (V. 274)

I am the end, my own Self, and nothing else. (V. 252)

The Self of man being beyond the law of causation is not a compound. (V. 256)

There is one Being, this Self; It neither comes nor goes. (III. 22)

The Self is all in all, none else exists. (IV. 393)

All we know is the projection of the Self. (VII. 93)

The Self in each of us is Brahman. (VII. 34)

I am the Infinite, that Eternal, Changeless. (II. 404)

If we enjoy everything in the Self, and as the Self, no misery or reaction will come. (II. 418)

In and through the Self all knowledge comes. (II. 305)

The Self of man is not the body, neither is It thought. (II. 233)

Self is in everything. (II. 318)

'I worship my Self' says the Advaitist. (II. 250)

I salute myself. (II. 250)

I am to worship, therefore, none but myself. (II. 250)

This Self or Soul or Substance is all that exists in the universe. (II. 274)

This Self is eternal and omnipresent. (II. 411)

The self is changeless. (II. 411)

The self-existent One is omnipresent, because He has no form. (II. 413)

The real self within me is also unknown and unknowable. (II. 458)

The Self—the Atman—is by Its own nature pure. (II. 249)

Whoever thinks that I am little makes a mistake, for the Self is all that exists. (II. 404)

Omnipresent is the Self of man. (II. 277)

The Self is that Peace which passeth beyond both evil and good. (VIII. 226)

Inside the heart, He has remained, the real Self. (VIII. 88)

The Self is beyond both freedom and bondage. (VIII. 35)

The Atman, Self, is the same as Brahman, the Lord. (VIII. 100)

This Self is all that is; It is the only reality. (VIII. 100)

Nothing exists but the Self; there is nothing else. (VIII. 101)

There is nothing to be asked for, desired for, beyond one's Self. (VIII. 504)

Happiness and misery are only in the senses, they cannot touch our real Self. (VIII. 10)

We *become* nothing; we *regain* our true Self. (VIII. 27)

The Self cannot be objectified. (VIII. 256)

All is the Self or Brahman. (VIII. 12)

The Self is the eternal subject. (VIII. 256)

My true Self is beyond all law. (VIII. 248)

When you can throw away *all*, only the true Self will remain. (VIII. 4)

Nothing else exists but the Self. (VIII. 195)

There is only one Self in the universe, only One Existence. (II. 461)

The Self is known, therefore, to everyone of us. (II. 305)

The Self can never be attached. (I. 464)

The Self is the essence of this universe, the essence of all souls; He is the essence of your own life, nay, 'Thou art That'. (I. 374)

The seer is really the Self, the pure one, the ever holy, the infinite, the immortal. (I. 238)

He conquers all who conquers self. (IV. 393)

A man must follow the tendencies peculiar to himself. (III. 358)

He who has more of this unselfishness is more spiritual and nearer to Shiva. (III. 143)

Each individual has to work out his own salvation. (V. 415)

The great thing is to have faith in oneself, even before faith in God. (V. 223)

You cannot believe in God until you believe in yourself. (V. 409)

## Self (I)

Self is the death of love. (V. 426)

Losing faith in one's self means losing faith in God. (III. 376)

Whenever you think of yourself you are bound to feel restless. (VI. 266)

This self is but the shadow of that real Self which is behind. (II. 417)

This little separate self must die. (II. 174)

All selfishness comes of holding on to the self, to this illusory self. (VIII. 98)

This little puny self must be sacrificed. (VIII. 24)

Our best work and our greatest influence is when we are without a thought of self. (VIII. 31)

He who gives up the little self for the world will find the whole universe his. (VIII. 336)

There is the real 'me' which nothing can destroy, and there is the phenomenal 'me' which is continually changing and disappearing. (VIII. 247)

Until we can free ourselves from nature, we are slaves; as she dictates so we must go. (I. 257)

Everyone has to get to the centre, however he may struggle to go back. (I. 422)

You make and mould your own life. (I. 497)

You are responsible for yourself. (I. 497)

We colour everything with our own selves. (I. 476)

We paint everything with ourselves. (I. 477)

I am already joined—from my very birth, from the very

fact of my life—I am in Yoga with that infinite life
and infinite goodness and infinite power. (III. 376)

I am that Infinite. (II. 471)

I am One, alone, through all eternity. (II. 472)

It is all my Self. (II. 472)

We never come nor go. We are where we are. (V. 410)

I am only existence and knowledge. (VIII. 525)

I am the master. (VIII. 522)

I am the Fear of fear, the Terror of terror, I am the fearless
secondless One; I am the Rule of destiny, the Wiper-
out of fact. (VIII. 522)

True Being is undifferentiated and *eternal*. (VI. 45)

Not being a compound, it will never die. (V. 256)

You were never born, and you will never die. (V. 257)

You are Omnipotent. (V. 51)

You are everywhere. (V. 271)

It is the Eternal Knower standing behind the whole
phenomena; He Himself is the phenomena. (III. 8)

The sky never changes: it is the cloud that is changing. (III. 9)

All knowledge is in me, all power, all purity, and all
freedom. (III. 130)

All power is within you; you can do anything and
everything. (III. 284)

We are everything, ready to do everything, we can do
everything, and man must do everything. (III. 376)

What can we not do ? (III. 244)

There is no help for you outside of yourself; you are the
creator of the universe. (III. 26)

It is not that you are going to become God or perfect;

you are already perfect; and whenever you think you are not, it is a delusion. (III. 16)

You are the permanent, the unchangeable. (III. 23)

You are where you are; these dreams, these various clouds move. (III. 23)

You are, by the grace of God and your own exertions, what you are. (III. 377)

You are He already. (III. 422)

You are the heirs of immortality, sons of the Eternal Father. (IV. 149)

The Kingdom of Heaven is within us. (IV. 246)

We cannot live satisfied where we are; that is the natural growth of the human soul. (IV. 194)

I am something higher than life. (IV. 232)

The superfine always eludes our view and laughs at our attempts to bring it down. (IV. 284)

[In meditation], for a moment, you can change this nature. (IV. 248)

We believe in a Personal God as the Christians do, but we go further: we believe that we are He! (IV. 191)

The less of this little 'I' the more of God there is in him. (IV. 174)

The 'I' has All become, the All is 'I' and Bliss. (IV. 395)

We are all in the dark; religion is to us a mere intellectual assent, a mere talk, a mere nothing. (II. 164)

None can die; none can be degraded for ever. (II. 402)

Darkness never existed, weakness never existed. (II. 295)

We are infinite. (VII. 98)

Oh, blessed am I! Freedom am I! I am the Infinite. (VII. 61)

All men are pure; all men are good. (VII. 420)

As a unity, it is free; as many, it is bound by law. (VII. 102)

Good and evil are our slaves, not we theirs. (VII. 13)

Without the 'I' there can be no 'you' outside. (VII. 101)

Nature, body, and mind go to death, not we; we never go
    nor come. (VII. 70)

We forge the chain, and we alone can break it. (VII. 54)

That which is nearest is least observed. (VII. 227)

You are free, free, free! (VII. 61)

Talk not of Yoga to make you pure; you are pure by your
    very nature. (VII. 73)

Everything will open up of itself. (VII. 254)

The eternal, the infinite, the omnipresent, the omniscient
    is a principle, not a person. (VII. 499)

We are infinite. (VII. 98)

We are the sons of fight and children of God. (V. 17)

This is the first fact of consciousness—I am. (II. 32)

It is all He, and all I, at the same time. (II. 322)

I am both death and life. (II. 414)

I ever was and ever am. (II. 404)

I am the pure and Blessed One. (II. 202)

It can never grow; It was always there, and only manifests
    Itself. (II. 228)

Everything is ours already—infinite purity, freedom,
    love, and power. (II. 296)

I am He, and he is I. (II. 251)

I am omnipresent, eternal. (II. 249)

I am beyond all life, beyond all death. (II. 251)

I am in everybody. (II. 469)

We are to take care of ourselves—that much we can do
    —and give up attending to others for a time. (II. 9)

There is nothing beyond me. (II. 415)

It is the unchangeable that is appearing as the changeable. (II. 344)

There is only One Being, One Existence, the ever-blessed, the omnipresent, the omniscient, the birth less, the deathless. (II. 236)

Where are you not? (II. 277)

We can do everything. (II. 294)

We are in reality that Infinite Being. (II. 339)

It is the greatest of all lies that we are mere men; we are the God of the universe. (II. 279)

You are already free and perfect. (II. 81)

You are not to be perfect, you are that already. (II. 82)

The great idea of which we here see the germ is that all these voices are inside ourselves. (II. 311)

As we understand these truths better, we find that the voice is in our own heart. (II. 311)

The infinite future is before you. (II. 225)

We are weak because we are ignorant. (II. 356)

The tiger in us is only asleep; it is not dead. (II. 364)

Every man and woman is the palpable, blissful, living God. (II. 326)

None comes and none goes. (II. 277)

The sky never changes; it is the clouds that change. (II. 280)

The worst lie that you ever tell yourself is that you were born a sinner or a wicked man. (II. 279)

None is great and none is small. (II. 399)

Thou alone art thy greatest enemy, thou alone art thy greatest friend. (II. 401)

The Divine Being was always within, the nearest of the near. (II. 401)

Every man exists, and every man must know, and every man is mad for love. (II. 458-59)

We are that eternal subject already; how can we know it ? (II. 82)

Everything in the universe is yours, stretch out your arms and embrace it with love. (II. 323)

It (Infinite) can never grow; It was always there, and only manifests itself. (II. 228)

The *real* 'I' cannot be grasped. (VIII. 3)

Find yourself bodiless. You never had a body. (VIII. 229)

You are what you are born. (VIII. 60)

Nothing is eternal except Himself. (VIII. 504)

Blessed are those who struggle to go beyond. (VIII. 341)

I am beyond, I am peace. (VII. 505)

Beyond all differentiation and combination, beyond space, time, and causation, I am that I am. (VIII. 249)

He (Brahman) is not born, he does not die, he is not in time and space. (VIII. 22)

We are lions in sheep's clothing of habit, we are hypno- tised into weakness by our surroundings. (VIII. 257)

Never does any help come from the outside. (VIII. 132)

In everybody I reside. (VIII. 129)

The universe is my body. (VIII. 129)

When I can enjoy through the whole universe, the whole universe my body. (VIII. 130)

I am the universe. (VIII. 101)

Say 'not', and you become 'not'; say 'is' and you become 'is'. (VIII. 22)

Our real nature is all bliss. (VIII. 7)

The real power, the real life, the real strength is in the unseen, the impersonal, the nobody. (VIII. 125)

I was, I am, and I will be. (VIII. 163)

I am He. (VIII. 163)

I am the whole mystery, God. (VIII. 225)

I am a body, the lower self; and I am the Lord of the universe. (VIII. 225)

You are divinities; the twinkling stars owe their existence to you. (VIII. 186)

You are the incarnations of the Almighty, Omnipresent, divine Principle. (VIII. 137)

The more I live, the more I become convinced every day that every human being is divine. (VIII. 186)

Our nature is joy, enjoyment, pleasure, and happiness. (VIII. 150)

You are all God. (II. 237)

You are the Self, the God of the universe. (II. 236)

We are all projected from one common centre which is God. (I. 416)

You are the almighty God playing. (II. 470)

Each of us is heir apparent to the Emperor of emperors; we are of the substance of God Himself. (III. 160)

We are God Himself though we have forgotten our own nature in thinking of ourselves as little men. (III. 160)

You are incarnations of God, all of you. (VIII. 137)

You are God and so am I; who obeys whom? (II. 320)

You are the God of the universe; where can you seek for help? (III. 26)

Therefore know that thou art He; thou art the God of this universe, *Tat Tvam Asi* (That thou art). (II. 236)

You are the whole of God. (II. 414)

Your godhead is the proof of God Himself. (II. 308)

You are the God of this universe. (I. 403)

We must become world-movers, for everything is in us. (III. 175)

What I have done, that I can undo. (III. 161)

Thou art the Reality. (VIII. 106)

You are the Infinite. (II. 462)

You are all infinite. (II. 470)

If you think that you are bound, you remain bound; you make your own bondage. (II. 462)

You are infinite; where is the place for you to go ? (II. 277)

You are the Pure One; awake and arise, O mighty one, this sleep does not become you. (II. 304)

You *have* everything, nay, you are everything. (II. 324)

You are the makers of your own fortunes. (II. 350)

You are never bound. (II. 470)

You are free already. (II. 470)

You can do anything and everything, you are almighty. (II. 300)

You know but little of that which is within you. (II. 302)

That is what you do when you cry after the joys of this world, for you do not know what true joy is. (II. 166)

You are not the slave of nature. (II. 182)

You are beyond the stars, the sun, and the moon. (II. 182)

Take the whole responsibility on your own shoulders, and know that you are the creator of your own destiny. (II. 225)

You are everywhere in the universe. (II. 235)

You were neither born, nor will you die. (II. 235)

You have had neither birth, nor will have rebirth, nor life, nor incarnation, nor anything. (II. 235)

In reality you are neither going nor coming, you are not being born, nor going to be reborn; you are infinite, ever-present, beyond all causation, and ever-free. (II. 235)

You are everywhere. (II. 235)

You are the omniscient, omnipresent being of the universe. (II. 235)

You are only one; there is only one such Self, and that One Self is you. (II. 235)

You are everywhere in the universe. (II. 235)

You are the Soul of this universe. (II. 237)

You are the Pure One, the Ever-blessed. (II. 237)

You and I are one. (II. 249)

That which is not the result of combination cannot die. (I. 251)

Everything is hidden by ourselves. (I. 477)

We do not become anything; we are what we are. (I. 512)

The body will die, but I shall not die. (I. 8)

It (Self) is beyond all law. (I. 238)

It (*Purusha*) does not exist, it is existence itself. (I. 249)

You are one with the universe. (I. 374)

You are not bound. (I. 500)

You are quite as great as Jesus, Buddha, or anybody else. (I. 483)

I am the one. (I. 501)

I am the Infinite. (I. 501)

I am the one Existence. Nothing else exists. I am everything. (I. 501)

You were never bound by laws; nature never had a bond for you. (I. 249)

We never change, we never die, and we are never
    born. (I. 419-20)

You are infinite. (I. 403)

You are all the world. (I. 461)

You are Infinite, deathless, birthless. (I. 461)

You gain nothing by becoming cowards. (I. 461)

Ye are not matter, ye are not bodies. (I. 11)

I have to accommodate myself to the world, and not the
    world to me. (I. 66)

We are responsible for what we are; and whatever we
    wish ourselves to be, we have the power to make
    ourselves. (I. 31)

The explanation of everything is after all in yourself. (I. 93)

Change of the unchangeable would be a contradic-
    tion. (I. 417)

When the whole universe sleeps, He sleeps not; He is
    working incessantly; all the changes and manifesta-
    tions of the world are His. (I. 80)

Anything that changes cannot be immortal. (I. 254)

I am free through eternity, I am never bound; I am the
    God of the universe through all eternity. (III. 28)

It is very easy to say, 'I am a *Jnani*', but very hard to be
    really one. (III. 27)

There is no God separate from you, no God higher than
    you, the real 'You'. (III. 24)

This One existence has to be realized. (III. 24)

The real *you* is already perfect, already strong. (III. 159)

We cannot *know* Brahman, but we are Brahman, the
    whole of It, not a piece. (VIII. 21)

Neither good nor bad, neither life nor death—only the
    one infinite Brahman exists. (II. 318)

The Brahman, the God of the Vedanta, has nothing outside of Himself, nothing at all. (I. 374)

All is Brahman, the One without a second. (III. 37)

Everything else is Maya, nothing else has real existence; whatever is of existence in any material thing is this Brahman. (III. 347)

Your Atman is the support of the universe—whose support do you stand in need of ? (IV. 279)

From the ant to the perfect man there is the same Atman in all, the difference being only in manifestation. (IV. 484)

The Atman is pure intelligence controlling and directing *Prana.* (VI. 128)

The Atman is the one unchangeable Truth. (VI. 519)

We are the Atman, deathless and free; pure, pure by nature. (V. 332)

In everyone is God, the Atman; all else is but dream, an illusion. (V. 417)

Atman is the reality of all. (VII. 75)

As Atman, we have no body. (VII. 104)

Always talk and hear and reason about this Atman. (VII. 121)

The Atman is the fearless. (VII. 29)

The sight of the Atman is the real vision of Jagannatha. (VII. 120)

The omnipresent Atman which depends on nothing else to support It is the only Refuge. (VII. 192)

The Atman never becomes the object. (VII. 33)

The Atman cannot be known by the mind for It is Itself the Knower. (VII. 199)

The Atman in bondage is called Jiva. (II. 258)

The Atman never comes nor goes, is never born nor dies. (II. 257-58)

Everything is a manifestation of the Atman. (II. 419)

All this universe is the reflection of that one Eternal Being, the Atman. (II. 249)

The Atman alone is free and that is our real essence. (VIII. 23)

The Atman is omnipresent. (VIII. 403)

This Atman is the Brahman itself. (III. 347)

Behind the mind is the Atman, the soul, the self of man. (III. 126)

Our Atman and soul are entirely different things. (II. 126)

Brahman is without action, Atman is Brahman, and we are Atman; knowledge like this takes off all error. (VII. 37)

(The) Atman knows neither happiness nor misery. (VIII. 28)

Both name and form is Atman, ever free. (IV. 393)

## Self-abnegation

The Lord has hidden Himself best, and His work is best; he who hides himself best, accomplishes most. (VII. 15)

Wherever we may begin we are sure to end in perfect self-abnegation. (I. 92)

The philosopher, the worker, and the devotee, all meet at one point, that one point being self-abnegation. (I. 86)

## Selfishness

Our own selfishness makes us the most arrant cowards; our own selfishness is the great cause of fear and cowardice. (III. 530)

Selfishness is the chief sin, thinking of ourselves first. (III. 143)

There should be no motive for selfishness. (III. 529)

Selfishness is the great curse of the world. (III. 529)

All selfishness is death, and this is true here or hereafter. (IV. 367)

With the sense of possession comes selfishness, and selfishness brings on misery. (I. 100)

There is no limit to this getting out of selfishness. (I. 109)

Selfish work is slave's work. (I. 57)

In all action the motive power is selfishness. (I. 477)

*That which is selfish is immoral, and that which is unselfish is moral.* (I. 110)

It is only selfishness that causes the difference between good and evil. (I. 90)

The exercise of might is invariably the exercise of selfishness. (I. 59)

**Self-knowledge**

When you know yourself you know all. (V. 411)

**Self-reliance**

The great thing is to have faith in oneself, even before faith in God; but the difficulty seems to be that we are losing faith in ourselves day by day. (V. 223)

**Self-restrained**

You do not require any assistance to govern yourself; you are already self-restrained. (III. 159)

**Self-sacrifice**

Self-sacrifice, indeed, is the basis of all civilization. (VII. 269)

**Self-surrender**

Complete self-surrender is the only way to spiritual illumination. (V. 258)

## Senses

Great is the tenacity with which man clings to the senses. (II.70)

The senses are all delusion. (I. 462)

We are bound by the senses; they play upon us, make fools of us all the time. (I. 516)

Our senses are limited, very limited indeed. (II. 156)

The senses cheat you day and night. (VII. 74)

Sense-happiness is not the goal of humanity. (III. 4)

## Service

Those who serve the servants of God are His greatest servants. (III. 142)

You cannot help anyone, you can only serve. (III. 246)

It is the greatest privilege in our life that we are allowed to serve the Lord in all these shapes. (III. 247)

Blessed are they whose bodies get destroyed in the service of others. (III. 83)

He who knows how to serve knows how to rule. (IV. 300)

The servant has no right to question. (IV. 131)

You work best when you work for others. (III. 276)

## Shakti

Without *Shakti* (power) there is no regeneration for the world. (VII. 484)

Without the grace of *Shakti*, nothing is to be accomplished. (VII. 484)

The worship of Mahavira must be introduced; the *Shakti-puja* must form a part of our daily practice. (V. 389)

Do you know who is the real '*Shakti*-worshipper'? It is he who knows that God is the omnipresent force in the universe and sees in women the manifestation of that Force. (V. 26)

## Shiva

If you are a real lover of Shiva, you must see Him in everything and in everyone. (III. 115)

## Shraddha

What we want is the *Shraddha*. (III. 319)

What makes one man great and another weak and low is this *Shraddha*. (III. 319)

## Shravana

*Shravana* not only means hearing from the guru, but also repetition to our own selves. (VII. 410)

## Silence

Spirit speaks unto spirit in silence, and yet in most unmistakable language. (III. 146)

Perfect silence is the best refutation. (V. 55)

## Simplicity

Simplicity is the secret. (V. 259)

## Sin

This is the only sin—to say that you are weak, or others are weak. (II. 308)

If there is any sin in the world, it is weakness. (III. 151)

Will sin cure sin, weakness cure weakness? (III. 237)

Without giving, he who eats and enjoys eating, enjoys sin. (IV. 10)

Loving others is virtue, hating others is sin. (V. 419)

Doing good to others is virtue (*Dharma*), injuring others is sin. (V. 419)

*The greatest sin is to think yourself weak.* (VII. 54)

It is not fitting that you think yourself a sinner. (II. 304)

He alone is a sinner who sees a sinner in another man. (II. 279)

## Sita

Sita has gone into the very vitals of our race. (III. 256)
She is there in the blood of every Hindu man and woman;
we are all children of Sita. (III. 256)

## Slave

Slave of the body, slave of the mind, slave of the world,
slave of a good word, slave of a bad word, slave of
passion, slave of happiness, slave of life, slave of
death, slave of everything! This slavery has to be
broken. (III. 25)
Slave wants power to make slaves. (IV. 368)
There is no use in being a slave. (IV. 6)
The slave never gets anything. (V. 251)
The slave and the tyrant are synonymous. (V. 14)
Slavery is slavery. (I. 500)
The more we say 'I and mine', the more slavery grows,
the more misery increases. (I. 100)

## Society

Human society is a graded organization. (I. 36)
*That society is the greatest, where the highest truths
become practical.* (II. 85)
*Society has to pay homage to Truth or die.* (II. 84)
Being of one mind is the secret of society. (III. 299)
Society is nothing but an aggregate of individuals. (VII. 412)

## Soldier

The soldier is only to obey and speak not. (IV. 355)
The soldier has no right to reason. (IV. 131)

## Solution

The solution of any problem can never be attained on
racial, or national, or narrow grounds. (III. 269)

Our solution is renunciation, giving up, fearlessness, and love, these are the fittest to survive. (III. 205)

## Soul

There is infinite life before the soul. (II. 153)

Soul is not a force, neither is it thought. (II. 232)

Life is short, but the soul is immortal and eternal. (III. 304)

All powers and all purity and all greatness—everything is in the Soul. (III. 334)

The ancient sages penetrated deeper and deeper until they found that in the innermost core of the human soul is the centre of the whole universe. (II. 157)

There is a soul which is unchanging. (II. 344)

The human soul never forgets its freedom and is ever seeking it. (II. 400)

I am omnipresent, eternal. (II. 249)

It is nature that is changing, not the soul of man. (II. 277)

True knowledge of the world means knowledge of the soul, metaphysics; and he (Hindu) wants to enjoy that life. (II. 186)

Truth is the nature of all souls. (II. 358)

The *Sat-Chit-Ananda*—Existence-Knowledge-Bliss Absolute—is the nature, the birthright of the Soul. (II. 194)

The soul is by its nature free. (II. 196)

The soul is one with Freedom, and the soul is one with Existence, and the soul is one with Knowledge. (II. 193-94)

When this body falls off, the soul lives on. (II. 268)

The soul is the only thing which is not composed of nature. (II. 456)

The soul is causeless, and from this follow all the great
      ideas that we have. (II. 196)

The highest heaven, therefore, is in our own souls. (II. 184)

The greatest temple of worship is the human soul.
      (II. 184)

The essential nature of the soul is unlimited. (II. 460)

The soul was never born and will never die. (II. 294)

This soul of man, being simple, must have been existing
      for ever. (II. 268)

The soul is beyond all laws, physical, mental and
      moral. (II. 282)

The soul has neither pleasure nor pain. (II. 457)

The universal soul is infinite. (II. 413)

The soul never changes. (II. 440)

All nature is working for the enjoyment and experience
      of the soul. (II. 457)

The Soul is beyond life and death. (V. 256-57)

Everything is in the soul. (III. 334)

Our prophet-soul is the proof of their prophet-
      soul. (II. 308)

All wisdom and all purity are in the soul already. (II. 168)

Every soul is infinite, therefore, there is no question of
      birth and death. (II. 78)

Each soul, therefore, is a part of God. (II. 429)

The soul is beyond time, space, and causality—therefore
      unlimited, omnipresent. (VIII. 10)

The soul cries ever, 'Freedom, O Freedom!' (I. 335)

The soul in itself is perfect. (I. 319)

Every soul, like every particle of matter, is perfectly
      dependent on the will of God. (I. 394)

Every soul is infinite. (III. 407)

Every soul is destined to be perfect, and every being, in the end, will attain the state of perfection. (III. 45)

The soul can only receive impulses from another soul, and from nothing else. (III. 45)

The soul never comes nor goes. (V. 68)

Each soul is a star, and all stars are set in that infinite azure, that eternal sky, the Lord. (V. 69)

My Soul is the highest ideal that I can have. (V. 253)

Each soul is a circle. (V. 271)

The soul is a circle whose circumference is nowhere (limitless), but whose centre is in some body. (V. 271)

Every soul is omnipresent, so where can it come or go? (V. 281)

I look behind and after and find that all is right, in my deepest sorrows there is a soul of light. (VIII. 168)

You are the soul of the universe and its body also. (II.462)

The soul is beyond life and death. (V. 256-57)

To believe blindly is to degenerate the human soul. (IV. 216)

The human soul is the repository of infinite wisdom; what external agency can illuminate it ? (IV. 431)

Unless you realize the soul; there is no freedom. (IV. 245)

You are the soul, the pure, the free, all the time; you are the Witness. (IV. 96)

*None* is really weak; the soul is infinite, omnipotent, and omniscient. (III. 193)

The soul of my soul is the only true existence. (VII. 427)

The soul never kills or is killed. (VII. 90)

Souls are without beginning and without end, and immortal by their very nature. (III. 125-26)

Power will come, glory will come, goodness will come, purity will come, and everything that is excellent will come when this sleeping soul is roused to self-conscious activity. (III. 193)

Each soul is potentially divine. (I. 257)

The human soul is eternal and immortal, perfect and infinite, and death means only a change of centre from one body to another. (I. 10)

You are souls immortal, spirits free, blest and eternal. (I. 11)

Every soul must disintegrate to become God. (I. 198)

The soul has no sex; why should it degrade itself with sex ideas? (I. 260)

The nature of the soul is eternal bliss. (I. 237)

I am the Soul, the ever free; (I) never was bound. (I. 502)

Soul is the only reality, and we have forgotten it. (I. 287)

The soul itself has no colouring. (I. 253)

The soul is separate from nature. (I. 253)

We cannot perceive the Soul, because it has got mingled up with nature, with the mind, with the body. (I. 234)

The Soul is not a compound; It is the only eternal simple in the universe, and as such, It cannot be born, It cannot die; It is immortal, indestructible, the ever-living essence of intelligence. (I. 234)

We all agree that souls are without beginning and without end, and immortal by their very nature; also that all powers, blessing, purity, omnipresence, omniscience are buried in each soul. (III. 125-26)

## Sound-symbols

Apart from the higher philosophic and religious value

of the Word, we may see that sound symbols play a
prominent part in the drama of human life. (I. 74)

## Spirit

Not matter but spirit. (IV. 351)

The spirit is omnipotent. (IV. 352)

All is spirit. (IV. 233)

You are all sons of God, immortal spirit. (IV. 146)

Spirit must see itself as spirit. (IV. 246)

The spirit must be realized, and that is practical
religion. (IV. 246)

The spirit can neither come nor go, it only changes its
plane of manifestation. (VII. 500)

Spirit is beyond space and time and is everywhere.
(VII. 7)

The spirit must be divine; and spirit understood as spirit
must not be made into a man. (II. 372)

The spirit is the goal, and not matter. (II. 39)

The apparent man is merely a struggle to express, to
manifest this individuality which is beyond; and
evolution is not in the Spirit. (II. 81)

Spirit is not in time, nor in space. (VIII. 18)

Spirit has no superstitions—it is beyond the vain desires
of the body. (VIII. 133)

We are all spirit. (VIII. 126)

That is the secret : To think that I am the spirit and not
the body. (II. 37)

That is the truth : you are the spirit, you are not
matter. (VIII. 112)

Our ideal is the spirit. (VIII. 72)

Spirit is beyond all time and space. (VIII. 27)

Everything is an expression of the spirit; the minds are so many mirrors. (VIII. 180)

The Spirit alone is infinite. (I. 341)

I (Atman) am a spirit living in a body. (I. 8)

The spirit will triumph in the long run. (III. 199)

The spirit is reflected in mind and in everything. (V. 273)

To quicken the spirit, the impulse must come from another soul. (III. 45)

## Spiritual

No other ideal can put into us the same mass of energy as the spiritual. (II. 66)

We want spiritual ideals before us, we want enthusiastically to gather round grand spiritual names. (III. 315)

*The more our bliss is within, the more spiritual we are.* (VII. 11)

Spiritual things are told not in the language of matter, but in the language of the spirit; the superfine in the language of the superfine. (III. 394)

Spiritual vitality can be given from one mind to another. (I. 511)

He who gives man spiritual knowledge is the greatest benefactor of mankind. (I. 52)

## Spirituality

Spirituality must conquer the West. (III. 277)

The mainspring of the strength of every race lies in its spirituality, and the death of that race begins the day that spirituality wanes and materialism gains ground. (II. 65)

Our backbone is spirituality. (III. 444)

Spirituality has been always in India. (III. 137)

We must keep a firm hold on spirituality, that inestimable gift handed down to us by our ancient forefathers. (III. 153)

Spirituality can be communicated just as really as I can give you a flower. (IV. 178)

Spirituality can never be attained until materiality is gone. (V. 416)

Because your thirst for spirituality has not come, therefore you are sitting idly. (VII. 194)

Spirituality is the true basis of all our activities in life. (I. 52)

Spirituality can never be attained unless all material ideas are given up. (I. 462)

The gift of spirituality and spiritual knowledge is the highest, for it saves from many and many a birth; the next gift is secular knowledge, as it opens the eyes of human beings towards that spiritual knowledge; the next is the saving of life; and the fourth is the gift of food. (V. 267-68)

## Strength

If it is strength, go down into hell and get hold of it. (I. 479)

The best guide in life is strength. (I. 134)

Strength, strength it is that we want so much in this life, for what we call sin and sorrow have all one cause, and that is our weakness. (I. 381)

Strength is the medicine that the ignorant must have when oppressed by the learned. (II. 201)

Strength, therefore, is the one thing needful. (II. 201)

Strength is the medicine for the world's disease. (II. 201)

Strength is the medicine which the poor must have when tyrannized over by the rich. (II. 201)

What this world wants today, more than it ever did before, is strength. (II. 198)

The remedy for weakness is not brooding over weakness, but thinking of strength. (II. 300)

This is the great fact: strength is life, weakness is death. (II. 3)

Strength is felicity, life eternal, immortal; weakness is constant strain and misery : weakness is death. (II. 3)

We want strength, strength, and every time strength. (III. 238)

What we need is strength, who will give us strength? (III. 238)

Strength is life, weakness is death. (V. 332)

Strength is in goodness, in purity. (V. 409)

All drift towards the strong. (IV. 479)

## Struggle

This struggle itself is the grandest and most glorious that man can make. (II. 66)

## Study

The real study is 'that by which we *realize* the unchangeable.' (V. 411)

## Success

The degree of unselfishness marks the degree of success everywhere. (V. 240)

## Superstition

No superstition. (I. 480)

Superstition is a great enemy of man, but bigotry is worse. (I. 15)

If superstition enters, the brain is gone. (III. 278)

## Surrender

In unhappiness, sorrow, death, and desolation, the Mother's child shall always remain fearless. (VII. 230)

To work I have the right. Mother knows the rest. (VIII. 513)

We are Her automata. She is wirepuller. (VIII. 517)

It is He that works. We are only the instruments. (VIII. 345)

Devotion to the mother is the root of all welfare. (VIII. 530)

## Sympathy

Without real sympathy we can never teach well. (VII. 99)

## Tantras

The purport of the Tantras is to worship women in a spirit of Divinity. (VII. 215)

## Tapasya

Working for the sake of others itself constitutes *Tapasya* (practice of austerity). (VII. 110)

Power comes of austerities. (VII. 110)

## Task

The great task is to revive the whole man, as it were, in order to make him the complete master of himself. (II. 35)

## Teaching

He alone teaches who has something to give, for teaching is not talking, teaching is not imparting doctrines, it is communicating. (IV. 177-78)

All teaching implies giving and taking. (IV. 178)

The first test of true teaching must be, that the teaching should not contradict reason. (II. 390)

Until the inner teacher opens, all outside teaching is in vain. (VII. 71)

None can teach another. (VI. 65)

None can teach you; none can make a spiritual man of you. (II. 385)

No one was ever really taught by another; each of us has to teach himself. (I. 93)

## Theist

Real theists cannot work. (V. 245)

## Theory

Doctrine is of no use except for gymnastics. (I. 484)

No theories ever made men higher. (II. 336)

## Thought

Thought is the finest and highest action of *Prana*. (I. 150)

Doing is very good, but that comes from thinking. (II. 86)

Difference is the first sign of thought. (II. 365)

Mere thoughts are like little wavelets. (VI. 134)

We are the heirs of good and evil thought. (VI. 134)

Every new thought must create opposition. (V. 137)

Even thinking the least good of others gradually instils into the heart the strength of a lion. (V. 382)

Thought is like a bubble rising to the surface. (VI. 129)

The thought is followed by the word, and the word by the form. (VI. 100)

We are what our thoughts have made us; so take care of what you think. (VII. 14)

If you have to think, think good thoughts, great thoughts. (VIII. 131)

What we think we tend to become. (VIII. 39)

What we think we become. (VIII. 19)

When this variation in thought is kept up, we must exist; and we need not quarrel because of that variety. (III. 131)

Whatever we shall be in the future will be the result of what we think and do now. (III. 45)

Whatever you think, that you will be. (III. 130)

In our little universe, this human mind, we see a thought arise. Whence it arises we do not know; and when it disappears, where it goes, we know not either. (III. 1)

By dint of hard work, thoughts may be silenced altogether. (I. 494)

Thought ceases in meditation; even the mind's elements are quite quiet. (I. 494)

Every thought in the mind has a form as its counter-part. (I. 73)

Thoughts can be guided and controlled. (I. 494)

Our thoughts make things beautiful, our thoughts make things ugly. (I. 441)

## Time

Time is infinite. (II. 403; IV. 126)

Time and space are infinite, and therefore have neither beginning nor end. (II. 427)

Time is in me, not I in time. (I. 502)

Doing the duty of the time is the best way. (V. 125)

Time, space, and causation are all within this nature. (III. 123)

Time is but the method of our thinking, but we are the eternally present tense. (VIII. 22)

## Tolerance

Tolerance only—we preach and perform. (VI. 285)

We are bound to bear and forbear. (VI. 372)

The world is waiting for this grand idea of universal toleration. (III. 187)

**Travelling**

Travelling is the best thing in life. (VIII. 343)

**Trust**

We trust Him when He works just our way. (VI. 150)

**Truth**

That which is true must be infinite and eternal. (I. 449)

Through truth everything is attained. (I. 189)

Truth has always been universal. (I. 329)

Truth alone triumphs, and this is true. (I. 502)

In truth everything is established. (I. 189-90)

We are always after truth, but never want to get it. (I. 439)

Stop creation and you know the truth. (I. 453)

Truth can never come to us as long as we are selfish. (I. 476)

Man wants truth, wants to experience truth for himself. (I. 128)

Truth requires no prop to make it stand. (I. 132)

Truth is heaven. Bigotry is hell. (VI. 123)

Truth is the fruit of realization; therefore seek it within the soul. (VI. 82)

It is truth alone that gives strength. (II. 201)

Truth is strengthening. (III. 225)

Truth is purity, truth is all-knowledge; truth must be strengthening, must be enlightening, must be invigorating. (III. 225)

The greatest truths are the simplest things in the world, simple as your own existence. (III. 225)

Great truths are simple because they are of universal application. (VI. 35)

Truth is purity, truth is all knowledge. (III. 225)

Truth itself is always simple. (VI. 35)

All truth is eternal. (II. 358)

Truth is nobody's property; no race, no individual can lay any exclusive claim to it. (II. 358)

Truth alone gives life. (II. 201)

Truth never dreams. (II. 251)

We have first to get a glimpse of truth. (II. 167)

Truth is often far from being 'comfortable'. (VIII. 14)

All is truth no doubt, but relative truth, different in degrees. (VII. 120)

Truth stands on its own evidence, it does not require any other testimony to prove it true, it is self-effulgent. (III. 47-48)

Truth is to be judged by truth and by nothing else. (VII. 101)

The truth is not what we see. (VIII. 107)

The truth is never lost. (VII. 428)

*Truth does not pay homage to any society, ancient or modern*. (II. 84)

One cannot serve the God of Truth who leans upon somebody. (V. 72)

Everything that makes for oneness is truth. (II. 304)

The Absolute truth is only one. (IV. 54)

Every vision of truth that man has, is a vision of Him and of none else. (II. 383)

Thought, word, and deed should be perfectly true. (IV. 10)

Truth will never ally itself with falsehood. (V. 418)

All will come to truth in the long run. (II. 253)

If truth is not there, what is the use of life? (II. 473)

Ignorance and bigotry can never crush truth. (VII. 422)

One word of truth can never be lost. (V. 57)

The children of truth *live for ever*. (V. 71)

Today or tomorrow or ages after, truth will conquer. (V. 51)

Nothing can resist truth. (V. 110)

Truth at length must inevitably prevail. (V. 188)

Truth must prevail in the end. (V. 418)

Truth always triumphs. (V. 57)

Truth triumphs if only one pursues a peaceful course. (VI. 329)

Truth alone triumphs, not falsehood. Through Truth alone lies the path of *Devayana*. (VI. 284)

Truth is within us. (II. 327)

The infinite truth is never to be acquired. It is here all the time, undying and unborn. (VIII. 135)

Whatever is truth will remain for ever; whatever is not, none can preserve. (VIII. 382)

Books may perish, nations may go down in a crash, but the truth is preserved. (VII. 428)

Truth cannot be partial; it is for the good of all. (VII. 60)

Truth will preach itself, it will not die for the want of the helping hands of me! (VII. 488)

All power of creation must stop, and then you know the truth at once. (I. 453)

Truth comes unto him who knows the secret of it. (VI. 88)

The truth can be learnt from the lowest individual, no matter to what caste or creed he belongs. (V. 209)

Truth must have no compromise. (VII. 70)

To accomplish anything, we must be willing to die for truth. (VIII. 45)

Everything can be sacrificed for truth, but truth cannot be sacrificed for anything. (V. 410)

Few only know the truth. (IV. 395)

Not from error to truth, nor from bad to good, but from truth to higher truth, from good to better, best. (IV. 371-72)

Truth comes to those alone who worship at her shrine for her sake only, without fear and without shopkeeping. (IV. 258)

Truth is to be found not in subtraction but in addition. (IV. 191)

Truth never comes where lust and fame and greed of gain reside. (IV. 394)

One progresses from a smaller to a greater truth. (V. 202)

If in this hell of a world one can bring a little joy and peace even for a day into the heart of a single person, that much alone is true. (V. 177)

## Unattached

Everyday we renew our determination to be un-attached. (II. 6)

The test of his (Sri Ramakrishna's) grace is—unattachment to lust or wealth. (VII. 263)

## Unhappiness

If I am unhappy, it has been of my own making, and that very thing shows that I can be happy if I will. (III. 125)

Unhappiness is the fate of those who are content to live in this world, born as they are. (II. 111)

## Unity

In the heart of things there is Unity still. (II. 153)

To realize this unity is the end and aim of all meditation, and this is what Yajnavalkya was trying to explain to Maitreyi. (II. 422)

Unity is the only thing that exists. (I. 432)

All reasoning ends only in finding Unity; so we first use analysis, then synthesis. (VIII. 12)

Unity is behind all. (V. 192)

Perfect unity is reached when man says, 'I and my Father are one'. (VI. 136)

Unity in variety is the plan of the universe. (II. 381)

All is Perfect Union and Perfect Bliss. (II. 154)

All variations are in One. (VIII. 6)

He who says he is different from others, even by a hair's breadth, immediately becomes miserable. (I. 374)

There is, therefore; but one Atman, one Self, eternally pure, eternally perfect, unchangeable, unchanged (II. 275)

All substances in the last analysis are one. (VI. 126)

It is one body, one mind, one soul throughout. (VIII. 129)

Love, Lover and the Beloved are really one. (VIII. 258)

Happiness belongs to him who knows this oneness, who knows he is one with this universe. (I. 374)

If you go deep enough, all will be seen as only variations of the One. (II. 153)

Everything in the universe is that One, appearing in various forms. (II. 461)

It is the one existence appearing in all these variations. (IV. 233)

Unity in variety is the plan of creation. (I. 41)

'Look not to variety,' says the Vedantist, 'go back to unity.' (I. 432)

Unity in variety is the plan of creation, individuality in universality. (VI. 114)

When a perfect unity is reached, that science has nothing more of principles to tell us. (VI. 10)

The end and aim of all science is to find the unity, the One out of which the manifold is being manufactured, that One existing as many. (I. 133)

He has not been divided, but only appears to be divided. (III. 8)

The difference between our lives is not in kind. (II. 297)

It is that One, manifesting Himself as many. (II. 304)

There is really no difference between matter, mind, and spirit. (V. 272)

Call it (unity) God, Love, Spirit, Allah, Jehovah—it is the same unity that animates all life from the lowest animal to the noblest man. (V. 192)

As manifested beings we appear separate, but as a reality we are one. (V. 257)

In the Absolute there is neither time, space, nor causation; It is all one. (II. 132)

All will meet at the centre. (VIII. 38)

A straight line, infinitely projected, must end in a circle. (I. 196)

That one is appearing in these various forms, and all these various forms give rise to the relation of cause and effect. (II. 345)

This manifoldness is like a dream. (II. 303)

The ideal cannot be finite. (II. 350)

There is this oneness, this solidarity of the whole universe. (II. 415)

There is only one life and one world, and this one life and one world is appearing to us as manifold. (II. 303)

Everywhere we are one. (II. 466)

Whatever exists is you. You are the Infinite. (II. 462)

Oneness includes all animals. (II. 297)

Oneness is the secret of everything. (II. 299)

We believe that we are He. (II. 502)

Whatever exists is One. (II. 345)

Whatever is, is One. (II. 16)

There is but One. (VII. 96)

Everything is that One, the difference is in degree and not in kind. (II. 297)

There is a oneness behind all creation. (V. 202)

'One without a second' can have no second. (VIII. 7)

Oneness alone is love and fearlessness; separation leads us to hatred and fear. (VIII. 24)

There is only one Individual, and each of us is That. (VIII. 24)

I am not that little man or little woman cut off from all else; I am the one universal existence. (VIII. 138)

There is but One, seen by the ignorant as matter, by the wise as God. (VIII. 429)

There is only one Power, whether manifesting as evil or good. (VII. 22)

Unity is the object of religion. (VII. 427)

There are not two things. (I. 504)

The highest creed is Oneness. (I. 341)

The whole of our lives is one; we are one, even in thought. (I. 373)

We are absolutely one; we are physically one, we are mentally one, and as spirit, it goes without saying, that we are one, if we believe in spirit at all. (I. 373)

In injuring another, I am injuring myself; in loving another, I am loving myself. (I. 364)

All this indeed is He : He is in the universe : He is the universe Himself. (I. 374)

Whatever be the name, they are all worshipping God. (VI. 50)

It is all *He* ! In the tiger and in Iamb, in the saint and sinner all *He* ! (VI. 303)

We are the children of the Almighty, we are sparks of the infinite, divine fire. (III. 376)

All are His children, His body, His manifestation. (III. 82)

All that is real in me is He; all that is real in Him is I. (I. 323)

That which is in every atom, everywhere present, the essence of all things, the God of this universe—know that thou art He, know that thou art free. (VI. 27)

We and He are one. (III. 129)

We *are* Brahman, we *are* immortal knowledge beyond the senses, we *are* Bliss Absolute. (VIII. 35)

We are He. (III. 129)

All this which we see around us is the outcome of that consciousness of the divine. (I. 388)

There is one Self, not many. That one Self shines in various forms. (VIII. 100)

All is Brahman. (VII. 34)

All is my Self. (VII. 61)

In every being He lives, through all minds He thinks. (I. 341)

That soul is strong that has become one with the Lord; none else is strong. (I. 381)

The reality of the external world and the reality of the internal world are one and the same. (I. 419)

He is the one existence. (IV. 237)

The one runs through all this seeming variety. (IV. 233)

Wherever there is love, wherever there is a spark of joy, know that to be a spark of His presence because He is joy, blessedness, and love itself. (IV. 129)

Everything that is joyful in this life is but a particle of that real joy. (II. 167)

I in Thee and Thou in me. (VIII. 345)

There is but one Being which the ignorant call the world. (III. 21)

There are neither three nor two in the universe; it is all one. (III. 21)

Take away the form and shape, and you and I are all one. (III. 347)

There is but one Soul throughout the universe, all is but One Existence. (III. 188)

As soon as we come to know each other, love comes, must come, for are we not one? (III. 241)

From the lowest worm that crawls under our feet to the noblest and greatest saints, all have this infinite power, infinite purity, and infinite everything. (III. 407)

We always perceive the one. (III. 21)

The whole world is one. (III. 446)

There is but one entity in the whole world. (III. 535)

The infinite oneness of the Soul is the eternal sanction of all morality. (III. 189)

This oneness is the rationale of all ethics and all spirituality. (III. 189)

There is but one life; one world, one existence. (II. 297)

In Him we are all one. (II. 381)

All minds are mine. (VIII. 129)

In me all me's I have. (VIII. 164)

There is no difference between man and man essentially, all being alike divine. (I. 388)

We are all equal. (VIII. 18)

We are all brothers. (II. 164; VIII. 124)

Man is man's brother because all men are one. (VIII. 101)

All are one, and to hurt one's brother is to hurt one's Self. (VIII. 238)

No one can separate himself from his brother. (VI. 83)

When you hurt anyone you hurt yourself, for you and your brother are one. (VI. 83)

In hurting anyone I am hurting myself, in loving anyone I am loving myself. (III. 129)

Not one can be happy until all are happy. (VI. 83)

Absolute non-differentiation is death. (I. 114)

We are that Infinite. (II. 402)

The Impersonal only can be Infinite. (II. 333)

It is impossible to divide infinity. (I. 402)

The omnipresent, the infinite, cannot be two. (II. 460)

There cannot be two infinites. (II. 431; III. 347)

There are no two in anything. (II. 297)

If you take away these two differences of name and form, the whole universe is one; there are no two, but one everywhere. (II. 249)

There is neither nature, nor God, nor the universe, only that one Infinite Existence. (II. 249)

Advaita will be the future religion of thinking humanity. (VIII. 348)

Advaita was the only way to save India from materialism. (II. 138)

This Advaita was never allowed to come to the people. (II. 138)

If man wants to be rational and religious at the same time, Advaita is the one system in the world for him. (III. 404)

Advaita is the basis of ethics. (V. 257)

The dry, abstract Advaita must become living—poetic —in everyday life. (V. 104)

Advaita had no antagonism with the various sects existing in India. (II. 141)

Advaitism is the last word of religion and thought. (VI. 415)

We must prove the truth of pure Advaitism in practical life. (VII. 162)

Advaita—the non-duality, the Oneness, the idea of the Impersonal God—is the only religion that can have any hold on any intellectual people. (II. 139)

Advaita has no quarrel. (II. 141)

When God is (sought) within, it is monism. (II. 463)

That which is qualityless must be one. (II. 461)

We are all born monists, we cannot help it. (III. 21)

Many a little makes a mickle. (VI. 426)

Every place is the temple of the Lord. (II. 318)

Nobody has rights; nobody separately exists. (II. 283)

If man's life is immortal, so also is the animal's. (II. 297)

His sun shines for the weak as well as for the strong. (II. 224)

The fire that burns the child also cooks the meal. (VI. 54)

Every particle seeking its own complement when it finds that it is at rest. (V. 426)

Each is great in his own place. (VII. 7)

We want to unite all the powers of goodness against all the powers of evil. (VI. 285)

The amoeba and I are the same. (II. 297)

All rivers flow into the ocean. (III. 97)

All radii lead to the centre. (VII. 98)

We are the Universal. (II. 419)

We are like little particles floating in one mass, and that mass is God. (II. 430)

One atom in this universe cannot move without dragging the whole world along with it. (III. 269)

Everyone is but a manifestation of that Impersonal. (III. 129)

We are like waves in the ocean; the wave is the ocean and yet not the ocean. (II. 398)

All things in the universe are of divine origin and deserve to be loved. (III. 92)

Equality is the sign of the free. (VIII. 18)

You are the all in all. (III. 9)

You are in all, and you are all. (III. 9)

You are the same whatever you do, and you cannot change your nature. (III. 161)

You are already that. (III. 16)

Every atom is trying to go and join itself to the next atom. (VI. 5)

It is only when one does not see another, does not feel another, when it is all one—then alone fear ceases, then alone death vanishes, then alone *Samsara* vanishes. (III. 417)

## Unselfishness

The whole idea of human life can be put into that one word, unselfishness. (I. 182)

Unselfishness is more paying, only people have not the patience to practise it. (I. 32)

Are you unselfish ? That is the question. (I. 93)

The goal of all nature is freedom, and freedom is to be attained only by perfect unselfishness; every thought, word, or deed that is unselfish takes us towards the goal, and, as such, is called moral. (I. 110)

All ethics, all human action and all human thought, hang upon this one idea of unselfishness. (I. 182)

The perfectly unselfish man is the most successful. (II. 45)

## Upanishad

Freedom, physical freedom, mental freedom, and spiritual freedom are the watchwords of the Upanishads. (III. 238)

The path of the Upanishads is the pure path. (VI. 87)

The Upanishads are the great mine of strength. (III. 238)

There is no religion of fear in the Upanishads; it is one of Love and one of Knowledge. (III. 231)

The Upanishadic literature is the most wonderful painting of sublimity that the world has. (III. 234)

The first step in getting strength is to uphold the Upanishads, and believe—'I am the Soul', 'Me the sword cannot cut; nor weapons pierce; me the fire cannot burn; me the air cannot dry; I am the Omnipotent, I am the Omniscient.' (III. 244)

## Urge

When one is thirsty, can one sit idle? (VII. 194)

## Vairagya

Do not go to the senses is the watchword of *Vairagya*. (III. 418)

**Variety**

Variation is the sign of life, and it must be there. (II. 364)

Variety is but phenomenal, ephemeral and apparent. (I. 432)

Variety in unity is necessary to keep man as man. (III. 359)

Variety ought to be preserved in everything; for as long as there is variety the world will exist. (III. 359)

**Vedanta**

Vedanta does not say, 'Give it up': it says, 'Transcend it'. (VIII. 130)

Vedanta formulates, not universal brotherhood, but universal oneness. (VIII. 129)

Vedanta teaches the God that is in everyone, has become everyone and everything. (VIII. 125)

The one central ideal of Vedanta is this oneness. (II. 297)

The Vedanta says, there is nothing that is not God. (II. 321)

The Vedantic idea is the infinite principle of God embodied in everyone of us. (VIII. 126)

Not only is Vedanta the highest philosophy in the world, but it is the greatest poem. (I. 499)

The Vedanta does not in reality denounce the world. (II. 146)

This Vedanta philosophy is not the outcome of meditation in the forest only. (II. 292)

The Vedanta was (and is) the boldest system of religion. (II. 113-14)

The Vedanta recognizes no sin, it only recognizes error. (II. 295)

The ideal of Vedanta is to know man as he really is. (II. 325)

Weakness has got to go before a man dares to become a Vedantist. (III. 386)

The first step for the pure Vedantist is to be *Abhih*, fearless. (III. 386)

Whether we are conscious of it or not, we think the Vedanta, we live in the Vedanta, we breathe the Vedanta, and we die in the Vedanta, and every Hindu does that. (III. 323)

The principles of religion that are in the Vedanta are unchangeable. (III. 121)

The Vedanta only can be the universal religion. (III. 250)

This Vedanta, the philosophy of the Upanishads, I would make bold to state, has been the first as well as the final thought on the spiritual plane that has ever been vouchsafed to man. (III. 322)

Vedanta in its highest form can alone spiritualize their social aspirations. (IV. 316)

The Vedanta philosophy is the foundation of Buddhism and everything else in India. (V. 279)

Our Vedanta is the assertion of freedom always. (V. 288)

The idea of the Vedanta is to harmonize all. (V. 279)

The Vedanta has no quarrel with Buddhism. (V. 279)

That plan briefly is to bring the Vedantic ideals into the everyday practical life of the saint or the sinner, of the sage or the ignoramus, of the Brahmin or the Pariah. (V. 217)

The Vedanta is the rationale of all religions. (V. 212)

Without the Vedanta every religion is superstition; with it everything becomes religion. (V. 212)

Vedanta declares that religion is here and now. (VI. 13)

I am a Vedantist; Sachchidananda—Existence-Knowledge-Bliss Absolute—is my God. (VI. 311)

Vedantism teaches that there is but one existence and one thing real, and that is God. (III. 536)

A real Vedantist must sympathize with all. (VII. 28)

## Vedas

There is no new religious idea preached anywhere which is not found in the Vedas. (VI. 105)

The Vedas are the only exponent of the universal religion. (VI. 181)

Veda means the sum total of eternal truths. (VI. 496)

Veda is of the nature of *Shabda* or of idea. (VI. 496)

All that is called knowledge is in the Vedas. (II. 169)

We are all brothers in the Vedas. (III. 373)

The Vedas are, in fact, the oldest sacred books in the world. (VI. 47)

## Vice

Whatever retards the onward progress or helps the downward fall is *vice*; whichever helps in coming up and becoming harmonized is *virtue*. (IV. 357)

## Vivekananda

I base my teaching on the great Vedantic truth of the sameness and omnipresence of the Soul of the Universe. (III. 194)

My religion means expansion, and expansion means realization and perception in the highest sense—no mumbling words or genuflections. (I. 332)

My stay—my guide in life—my refuge—my friend—my teacher—my God—my real Self, Thou wilt never leave me, *never*. (VI. 303)

My motto is to learn whatever good things I may come across anywhere. (VI. 234)

Only one kind of work I understand, and that is doing good to others; all else is doing evil. (VI. 310-11)

I like boldness and adventure and my race stands in need of that spirit very much. (VIII. 531)

I am the Advaitist; our goal is *knowledge*—no feelings, no love, as all that belongs to matter and superstition and bondage. (VIII. 525)

For all time my head shall bend low in reverence wherever I see greatness, broadness of heart, and holiness. (VI. 210)

I see clear as daylight that there is the one Brahman in all, in them and me—one *Shakti* dwells in all. The only difference is of manifestation. (VII. 246)

Individuality is my motto. (VII. 487)

I seek no help. I reject none. (VII. 487)

I only say, awake, awake! (VII. 501)

*I will stand by you unto death* whether you work for India or not, whether you give up Vedanta or remain in it. (VII. 512)

My hope of the future lies in the youths of character—intelligent, renouncing all for the service of others, and obedient—who can sacrifice their lives in working out my ideas and thereby do good to themselves and the country at large. (VII. 230)

Mother's grace, Mother's blessings are all paramount to me. (VII. 484)

My ideal indeed can be put into a few words and that is : to preach unto mankind their divinity, and how to make it manifest in every movement of life. (VII. 501)

Come what may, I must attain my ideal first. (VII. 126)

Come what may, I shall not forget my duty, whether the world remains or dissolves—these are the words of a great hero. (VII. 226)

I am born to proclaim to them that fearless message— 'Arise, Awake !' (VII. 182)

I hate only one thing in the world—hypocrisy. (VII. 465)

I have found the pearl for which I dived into the ocean of life. (VIII. 538)

Alone and drifting about in the will-current of the Mother has been my whole life. (VIII. 517)

I am attaining peace that passeth understanding, which is neither joy nor sorrow, but something above them both. (VIII. 504)

'I reject the Vedas!' is the last word of the Vedanta philosophy. (VIII. 255)

I have never retreated in a fight. (VIII. 430)

I want my work to be quick like lightning, and firm as adamant. (VIII. 430)

'India, with all thy faults I love thee still.' (VIII. 327)

I am doing the Lord's work, and wherever He leads I follow. (VIII. 328)

I love my God, my religion, my country. (VIII. 331)

I love the poor, the ignorant, the downtrodden, I feel for them—the Lord knows how much. (VIII. 331)

Only let me be perfectly pure, perfectly sincere, and perfectly unselfish. (VIII. 336)

The upshot of the whole thing is—I want bold, daring, adventurous spirits to help me. Else I will work alone. I have a mission to fulfil. I will work it out alone. (VIII. 366)

I shall have one man only to follow me, but he must be true and faithful unto death. (VIII. 372)

I do not care for success or no success. (VIII. 372)

I must keep my movement *pure* or I will have none. (VIII. 372)

When I think 'I am Brahman', then I alone exist. (VIII. 385)

You need not be afraid, I do not work alone, but He is always with me. (VIII. 397)

In my eyes this world is mere play—and it will always remain as such. (VIII. 431)

I am a man of action. (VIII. 431)

I am the child of the Divine Mother, the source of all power and strength. (VIII. 432)

To me, cringing, fawning, whining, degrading inertia and hell are one and the same thing. (VIII. 432)

I pray that I may not have to die a coward. (VIII. 432)

I am in a tremendous hurry, I want to work at hurricane speed, and I want fearless hearts. (VIII. 432)

Work I want—I don't want any humbug. (VIII. 439)

I want work, I want vigour—no matter who lives or dies. (VIII. 469)

My mission is to obey and work. He knows the rest. (VIII. 501)

'The greatest thing I can obtain is my Self.' (VIII. 504)

'I am free', therefore I require none else for my happiness. (VIII. 504)

'Alone through eternity, because I was free, am free, and will remain free for ever.' (VIII. 504-05)

'Alone, alone, I am the one without a second.' (VIII. 505)

I have no good to attain, no ideal to clench up to, no ambition to fulfil; I, the diamond mine, am playing with pebbles, good and evil. (VIII. 505)

I am Peace that passeth understanding; understanding only gives us good or evil. (VIII. 505)

No more materialism, no more this egoism, I must become spiritual. (VIII. 118)

My first reverence is to the guru. (VIII. 112)

My dearest and nearest relative in life is my guru. (VIII. 112)

Let character be formed and then I shall be in your midst. (VI. 293)

Even if a thousand births have to be taken in order to relieve the sorrows of the world, surely I will take them. (VI. 502)

May the Lord break the bondage of all—may all come out of Maya—is the constant prayer of Vivekananda. (VI. 359)

My idea is to bring to the door of the meanest, the poorest, the noble ideas that the human race has developed both in and out of India, and let them think for themselves. (V. 28-29)

Whatever I do, I try my best to avoid publicity. (V. 25)

I am a hater of celebrity. (V. 21)

Day by day I am feeling that the Lord is with me, and I am trying to follow His direction. (V. 23)

I may perish of cold or hunger in this land, but I bequeath to you, young men, this sympathy, this struggle for the poor, the ignorant, the oppressed. (V. 16)

I must stick to my guns, life, or death. (V. 12)

I am determined, and I have a call from Above; I see no way, but His eyes see. (V. 12)

'I look upon religion as the innermost core of edu-cation.' (V. 231)

My faith is in the younger generation, the modern generation, out of them will come my workers. (V. 223)

I consider that the great national sin is the neglect of the masses, and that is one of the causes of our downfall. (V. 222)

I believe the Indian nation is by far the most moral and religious nation in the whole world. (V. 220)

My watchword is construction, not destruction. (V. 217)

Since I have nothing whatever to do with ritual or dogma; my mission is to show that religion is everything and in everything. (V. 202)

I call upon men to make themselves conscious of their divinity within. (V. 187-88)

I direct my attention to the individual, to make him strong, to teach him that he himself is divine. (V. 187)

My teaching is antagonistic to none. (V. 187)

Know this for certain that my love can never cease. (V. 161)

The power behind me is not Vivekananda but He the Lord, and He knows best. (V. 137)

May I be born again and again, and suffer thousands of miseries so that I may worship the only God that exists, the only God I believe in, the sum total of all souls—and above all, my God the wicked, my God the miserable, my God the poor of all races, of all species, is the special object of my worship. (V. 137)

My ambition is to be a conscious dreamer, that is all. (V. 100)

What I want is muscles of iron and nerves of steel, inside which dwells a mind of the same material as that of which the thunderbolt is made. (V. 117)

I have a truth to teach, I, the child of God. (V. 93)

Fear not, my soul ! Be alone. (V. 72)

Be still, my soul ! Be alone ! and the Lord is with you. (V. 72)

The present looks very gloomy indeed; but I am a fighter and must die fighting, not give way. (VI. 420)

My resolve is something like either to lay down my life or realize my ideal. (VI. 216)

May I never, never seek for help from any being but Thee. (VI. 303)

My *idea* and all my life with it—and to *God* for help; to none else! (VI. 302)

Whether I live or die, whether I go back to India or not, remember this specially, that universality—perfect acceptance, not tolerance only—we preach and perform. (VI. 285)

I (Vivekananda) am not the standard of the universe. (I. 66)

I may die here unsuccessful; another will take up the task. (V. 17)

Let the world come, the hells come, the gods come, let Mother come, I fight and do not give in. (VI. 421)

My salutation goes to the feet of the good, the saintly, and to the feet of the wicked and the devilish! (II. 34)

I believe in reason and follow reason. (II. 336)

I do not believe in reform; I believe in growth. (III. 213)

Theirs is the method of destruction, mine is that of construction. (III. 213)

My idea is growth, expansion, development on national lines. (III. 195)

I want the intensity of the fanatic plus the extensity of the materialist. (III. 174)

I am the teacher of virtue, not of sin. (III. 240)

I glory in being the preacher of light, and not of darkness. (III. 240)

I do not want a crowd. (IV. 58)

Struggle, struggle, was my motto for the last ten years. Struggle, still say I. (IV. 367)

Sri Ramakrishna used to say, 'As long as I live, so long do I learn.' (IV. 477)

Let me die a true *Sannyasin* as my master did, heedless of money, of women, and of fame. (V. 413)

Know for certain that the work done by me is not the work of Vivekananda, it is His work—the Lord's own work ! (V. 358)

God of Truth, be Thou alone my guide ! (V. 71)

I shall inspire men everywhere, until the world shall know that it is one with God. (V. 414)

Fear is the greatest sin my religion teaches. (V. 71)

I shall work incessantly until I die, and even after death I shall work for the good of the world. (V. 64)

I am poor, I love the poor. (V. 58)

I believe in helping the miserable. (V. 52)

I believe in going even to hell to save others. (V. 52)

I believe in God and I believe in man. (V. 52)

However sublime be the theories, however well-spun may be the philosophy—I do not call it religion so long as it is confined to books and dogmas. (V. 50)

I do not believe in a God or religion which cannot wipe the widow's tears or bring a piece of bread to the orphan's mouth. (V. 50)

My whole ambition in life is to set in motion a machinery which will bring noble ideas to the door of everybody, and then let men and women settle their own fate. (V. 29)

Purity, perseverance and energy—these three I want. (VI. 342)

## Want

Want is that without which we cannot live. (IV. 19)

Wants are being multiplied. (VI. 53)

Want makes us beggars and we are sons of the king, not beggars. (VII. 35)

## Weakness

It is not fitting that you think yourself weak. (II. 304)

If you think yourselves strong, strong you will be. (III. 130)

The weak have no will, and can never work. (IV. 58)

He who always thinks of himself as weak will never become strong, but he who knows himself to be a lion. (VI. 311)

I cannot be miserable unless I am weak. (I. 426)

The sign of death is weakness. (I. 479)

There is only one sin. That is weakness. (I. 479)

All weakness, all bondage is imagination. (I. 479)

The only saint is that soul that never weakens, faces everything, and determines to die game. (I. 479)

We suffer because we are weak. (II. 198)

Weakness is the one cause of suffering. (II. 198)

We lie, steal, kill and commit other crimes, because we are weak. (II. 198)

We die because we are weak. (II. 198)

We become miserable because we are weak. (II. 198)

Weakness leads to slavery. (II. 3)

Weakness leads to all kinds of misery, physical and mental. (II. 3)

There are two curses here: first our weakness, secondly, our hatred, our dried up hearts. (III. 432)

Weakness is sin. (VI. 474)

## Wealth

Wealth does not belong to anybody. (II. 148)

## Western

All this Western pomp is only vanity, only bondage of the soul. (VI. 359)

The Western is looking up outside for his God. (III. 375)

To the Western their religious books have been inspired, while with us our books have been expired. (III. 375)

## Wickedness

Wickedness is ignorance, weakness. (VI. 141)

## Wife

The wife is the centre of a circle, the fixity of which depends upon her chastity. (VIII. 198)

## Will

The will is almighty. (II. 356)

It is will that is the power. (III. 299)

The will is stronger than anything else. (III. 224)

A pure and a strong will is omnipotent. (III. 224)

The human will stands beyond all circumstance. (III. 125)

It is will that moves the world. (V. 47)

## Witness

The witness alone enjoys, and none else. (III. 419)

The more and more you are the witness of anything in
life, the more you enjoy it. (III. 419)

## Woman

Woman is as courageous as man. (II. 26)

If a woman is a jewel, take her in marriage even if she
comes from a low family of the lowest caste.
(III. 152)

The women of India must grow and develop in the
footprints of Sita, and that is the only way. (III. 256)

The paramount duty of a woman is to serve her husband
by thought, word, and deed. (VI. 247)

If you do not raise the women, who are the living
embodiment of the Divine Mother, don't think that
you have any other way to rise. (VII. 214)

That country and that nation which do not respect women
have never become great, nor will ever be in future.
(VII. 215)

The ideal of womanhood in India is motherhood—that
marvellous, unselfish, all-suffering, ever-forgiving
mother. (VIII. 58)

Words charged with spirit have wonderful power.
(VI. 89)

Any action that makes us go Godward is a good action,
and is our duty. (I. 64)

Any action that you do for yourself will bring its effect
to bear upon you. (I. 87)

All good acts tend to make us pure and perfect. (I. 76)

There cannot be any action which is perfectly pure, or
any which is perfectly impure. (I. 83)

## Word

Words are only a mode of mind acting on mind. (VI. 134)

Every word is the power of God. (III. 513)

## Work

To work we have the right, the result is in the hands of Lord. (IV. 408)

The law of *Karma* can never be hoodwinked. (VIII. 88)

He who in good action sees that there is something evil in it, and in the midst of evil sees that there is something good in it somewhere, has known the secret of work. (I. 83)

Blessed are we that we are ordered out here. (I. 103)

He who does the lower work is not therefore a lower man. (I. 66)

Intense activity is necessary; we must always work. (I. 34)

Activity is the manifestation of inferior strength, calmness, of the superior. (I. 202)

Never will unhappiness or misery come through work done without attachment. (I. 77)

Work is inevitable, it must be so; but we should work to the highest purpose. (I. 99)

Man work with various motives. There cannot be work without motive. (I. 31)

Even the lowest forms of work are not to be despised. (I. 33)

Every one must work in the universe. (I. 98)

He (man) works best who works without any motive. (I. 117)

When you are doing any work, do not think of anything beyond. (I. 71)

To work properly, therefore, you have first to give up the idea of attachment. (I. 88)

The greatest work is done only when there is no selfish motive to prompt it. (I. 66)

The main effect of work done for others is to purify ourselves. (I. 84)

When work will become worship—nay, something higher—then will work be done for its own sake. (I. 66)

All work is simply to bring out the power of the mind which is already there, to wake up the soul. (I. 31)

He works, who has nothing to gain from work. (II. 149)

He works, who has no ulterior motive in view. (II. 149)

He is already in every work, in every thought, in every feeling. (II. 150)

All our actions in this world will determine our future birth. (II. 256)

Our only work is to arouse this knowledge in our fellow-beings. (II. 358)

Our actions are but effects. (II. 15)

We have to work, constantly work with all our power. (II. 1)

The calmer we are, the better for us, and the more the amount of work we can do. (II. 293)

We have bound ourselves by our own actions. (II. 257)

You only get what you deserve. (II. 367)

Real activity, which is the goal of Vedanta, is combined with eternal calmness. (II. 292-93)

Every action and every thought that helps the Jiva to expand, to manifest its real nature, is good. (II. 348)

If we stand still, we die. (III. 195)

Whatever we are now is the result of our acts and thoughts in the past. (III. 45)

The more you work to help others, the more you help yourselves. (III. 134)

Millions of your ancestors are watching, as it were, every action of yours, so be alert. (III. 152)

We must do our duty for duty's sake, not for the hope of reward. (IV. 191)

You cannot take a man with pitchfork and push him up there; we all have to work up gradually. (IV. 36)

Ours is to work. The results will take care of themselves. (IV. 353)

Work out what you feel and let the world see. (IV. 420)

One falls, and another takes up the work. (V. 17)

We will do great things for the world, and that for the sake of doing good and not for name and fame. (V. 23)

You are all *born to do it*. (V. 30)

Blessed are we that we are given the privilege of working for Him, not of helping Him. (V. 246)

Every action of man is worship. (V. 291)

That work alone brings unattachment and bliss, wherein we work as masters of our own minds. (V. 241)

Work for a motive brings misery. (V. 241)

No great things were ever done without great labour. (V. 12)

To work without motive, to work unattached, brings the highest bliss and freedom. (V. 249)

Like smoke round the fire, some evil always clings to work. (V. 248)

There is no good work that has not a touch of evil in it. (V. 248)

All work has its ups and downs, its periods of intensity and slackness. (V. 161)

Every work has got to pass through hundreds of difficulties before succeeding. (V. 104)

Work incessantly, but see something behind the work. (VI. 84)

Every great work is done slowly. (VI. 323)

Work will produce more work. (VI. 57)

Every action that helps a being manifest its divine nature more and more is *good*, every action that retards it is *evil*. (VI. 319)

Work always brings evil with it. (VIII. 517)

Work, work, work—I care for nothing else. Work, work, work, even unto death ! (VI. 400)

Work, work—live the life; what do doctrines and opinions count? (VI. 403)

Disinterested work is quite as difficult as *Tapasya*. (VII. 111)

No work succeeds by condemnation. (VII. 221)

External motion we call action; internal motion is human thought. (VII. 421)

No work is petty. (VII. 508)

Work done for the Self gives no bondage. (VII. 63)

Work Purifies the heart and so leads to *Vidya* (wisdom). (VII. 39)

Work or worship is to bring you back to your own nature. (VII. 54)

Action can never die without producing action. (VIII. 236)

The best work is only done by alternate repose and work. (VIII. 448)

All work should be done without any desire to enjoy the fruits thereof. (VIII. 153)

A work can be judged by its results only. (VIII. 411)

All work is spoilt by dilatoriness. (VIII. 412)

Slow, persistent and silent work does everything. (VIII. 382)

Great work requires great and persistent effort for a long time. (VIII. 383)

'Every deed returns to the doer'. (VIII. 16)

That which is limited is material. (I. 341)

First, believe in this world—that there is meaning behind everything. (I. 441)

We are responsible for what we are. (I. 31)

The law of *Karma* means the law of causation, of inevitable cause and sequence. (I. 94)

*Karma* is the eternal assertion of human freedom. (V. 213)

Whatever helps the manifestation of Brahman is good work. (VII. 221)

Each one of us is in the hands of *Karma*; it works itself out. (V. 144)

It is *Karma* that brings us together, and *Karma* separates. (VIII. 478)

Karma-yoga means even at the point of death to help any one, without asking questions. (I. 62)

Now is wanted—as said in the *Gita* by the Lord—intense Karma-yoga, with unbounded courage and indomitable strength in the heart. (VII. 185)

The watchword of the *Karma-yogi* is 'not I, but Thou'. (VIII. 153)

## World

The whole world is full of the Lord. (II. 146)

All the world is my country, the whole universe is mine, because I have clothed myself with it as my body. (II. 283)

This world is nothing. Beyond this world is something which is very real. (II. 144)

The world vanishes in a moment and is gone. (II. 71)

We see the world as we are. (II. 87)

This world is too full of blustering talk. We want a little more earnest work, and less talk. (II. 380)

Understand what this world is, so that it may not hurt you. (II. 312)

Everything is bound by *Karma*. (I. 450)

Woe unto the world when everyone is of the same religious opinion and takes to the same path. (III. 131)

The world is just a playground, and we are here having good fun, having a game. (III. 94)

We must die, that is certain; let us die then for a good cause. (III. 446)

This world is a means to an end, and not an end itself. (IV. 8)

This world is neither good nor evil. (IV. 207)

Worlds must disappear in the soul like drops in the ocean. (IV. 240)

The whole world is full of God and not of sin. (V. 413)

This is the school of misery, which is also the school for great souls and prophets for the cultivation of sympathy, of patience, and, above all, of an indomitable iron will which quakes not even if the universe be pulverized at our feet. (V. 15-16)

This earth is higher than all heavens; this is the greatest school in the universe. (V. 94)

This very world is seen by the five senses as matter, by the very wicked as hell, by the good as heaven, and by the perfect as God. (V. 272)

Praise and censure have no value in this world of ours. (V. 330)

This world does not exist outside. It is all a mental projection. (VI. 487)

This world *is* and *is not—manifold yet one*. (VI. 226)

*Jagat* (world) means that which is moving. (VI. 110)

This world will be world ever and always. What we are, so we see it. (VI. 371)

The progress of the world means more enjoyment and more misery too. (VI. 380)

There is no world. It is God Himself. In delusion we call it world. (VI. 371)

The world is a form of our thoughts. (VI. 115)

This world is not for cowards. (VI. 83)

This world is neither true nor untrue, it is the shadow of truth. (VII. 11; VIII. 30)

In this world everything depends upon one's words. (VII 445)

The world has no absolute reality which only belongs to Brahman, which is beyond the reach of mind and speech. (VII. 228-29)

It is not creation, but manifestation. (VII. 424)

No two people see the same world. (VII. 74)

The world for me, not I for the world. (VII. 13)

This is the world my brother—this illusion of Maya—the Lord alone is true. (VII. 500)

This world is our friend when we are its slaves and no more. (VIII. 366)

This world will always be a mixture of good and evil, of happiness and misery; this wheel will ever go up and come down; dissolution and resolution is the inevitable law. (VIII. 341)

The whole world is full of God and not of sin. (VIII. 219)

The universe is a cobweb; minds are spiders. (VIII. 225)

This world is not for our sake. (I. 88)

The whole world is for man. (I. 491)

This world will always continue to be mixture of good and evil. (I. 80)

The universe is a fact; and if a fact, it is a huge composite of good and evil. (VI. 147)

The whole universe is a play of differentiation and oneness; the whole universe is a play of the finite in the Infinite. (I. 433)

The whole universe is composed of subtle vibrations. (I. 151)

God is true. The universe is a dream. (I. 501)

The whole universe is a play of unity in variety, and of variety in unity. (I. 433)

All that we see in the universe has for its basis this one struggle towards freedom. (I. 108)

When the whole universe sleeps, He sleeps not. (I. 80)

This whole universe is only one speck of the Infinite being. (I. 96)

The world is neither good nor bad; the world is the world. (I. 515)

This world is neither good nor evil. (I. 75)

This world is like a dog's curly tail. (I. 79)

That this world is created for our enjoyment is the most wicked idea that holds us down. (I. 88)

This world is only one drop in an infinite ocean, one link in an infinite chain. (I. 182)

It is much more difficult to live in the world and worship God than to give it up and live a free and easy life. (I. 42)

This world is a play. You are His playmates. Go on and work, without any sorrow, without any misery. (I. 441)

Everything in the world is good, is holy and beautiful. (I. 441)

Beyond this world is something which is very real. (II. 144-45)

The whole world is one. (III. 129)

Worldly people love life. (III. 446)

The whole universe is in fact the result of this struggle for freedom. (I. 108)

The whole universe, therefore, is a unit, from whatever standpoint you view it. (II. 32)

The universe is one, whatever point you touch. (I. 507)

The whole universe is one person; let go the little things. (II. 323)

The whole of this universe is one Unity, one Existence, physically, mentally, morally and spiritually. (II. 249)

The whole universe is all one in the Self which is called Brahman. (II. 461)

The whole universe is one existence. (VIII. 138)

This whole universe is that one Unit Existence; name and form have created all these various differences. (II. 275)

The whole universe is really one. (I. 420)

Throughout the universe is a unity (at bottom). (I. 507)

The whole universe is a vast play. (II. 470)

This universe itself is the Absolute, the unchangeable, the noumenon. (II. 338)

The universe is ever hurrying on to return to that state of equilibrium again. (II. 273)

The universe is our body. (VIII. 27)

Name and form constitute the universe. (VIII. 277)

The whole universe is imagination, but one set of imaginations will cure another set. (V. 266)

The universe is really homogeneous. (VI. 125)

The universe is all built on the same plane. (VI. 41)

There is both change and changeless in this universe. (II. 274)

This universe is a constant prayer. (VIII. 102)

The universe is—objectified God. (V. 409)

Everything must be sacrificed, if necessary, for that one sentiment, *universality*. (VI. 285)

Every phenomenon that we can see, feel, or think of, is finite, limited by our knowledge, and the personal God as we conceive of Him is in fact a phenomenon. (II. 338)

This earth is called the *Karma-Bhumi*; the sphere of *Karma*. (II. 270)

This earth, therefore, is the *Karma-Bhumi*; it is this earth from which we attain to liberation. (III. 127)

Everything moves in a circle; a straight line, infinitely produced, becomes a circle. (II. 231)

Everything must complete the circle, and come back to its source. (II. 231)

Going back to the finer form is all that is meant by destruction. (II. 443)

Everything is in a state of flux. (I. 412)

## Worship

The highest worship is that of the man who loves God for God's sake. (I. 440)

Worship is feeling the holiness of God. (II. 478)

External worship is only a symbol of internal worship; but internal worship and purity are the real things. (III. 141)

Worship is constant remembering as may be seen from the essential texts of scriptures. (III. 35)

This is the gist of all worship—to be pure and to do good to others. (III. 141)

The first of all worship is the worship of the *Virat*—of those all around us. (III. 301)

Worship is valid and leads to the goal if the heart is pure and the heart is sincere. (III. 261-62)

Everything is useless except the worship of the Lord and the Lord alone. (III. 354)

You must see that every worship is given unto Him whatever may be the name or the form. (III. 115)

He who sees Shiva in the poor, in the weak, and in the diseased, really worships Shiva; and if he sees Shiva only in the image, his worship is but preliminary. (III. 142)

We must worship the beautiful for beauty's sake, not for the hope of reward. (IV. 191)

Never, really, was there ever worship of anything but the spirit by man. (VI. 60)

This indeed is worship,—worship of the Lord in the human tabernacle, '*nedam yadidam upasate*—not this that people worship'. (VI. 401)

Worship is everywhere, in every soul. (VI. 50)

Everyone worships God. Whatever be the name, they are all worshipping God. (VI. 50)

Every worship consists of prayer in the highest form. (VI. 110)

Let the Vedas, the Koran, the Puranas, and all scriptural lumber rest now for some time—let there be worship of the visible God of Love and Compassion in the country. (VI. 410)

Ceremonials are the lowest form; next God external, and after that God internal. (VII. 60)

Repeating the *Om* continually is the only true worship. (VII. 62)

## Yoga

Non-attachment is the basis of all the Yogas. (I. 101)

Freedom of the soul is the goal of all Yogas. (I. 55)

Yoga changes the body. (I. 224)

Yoga is the science which teaches us how to get these perceptions. (I. 127)

The aphorisms of Patanjali are the highest authority on Raja-yoga, and form its text book. (I. 122)

Yoga can only be safely learnt by direct contact with a teacher. (I. 123)

The whole theory of Yoga is to go beyond the mind. (VI. 128)

Yoga means 'yoke', 'to join', that is, to join the soul of man with the supreme Soul or God. (VIII. 36)

The end and aim of Yoga is to realize God. (VI. 124)

## Yogi

A Yogi must avoid the two extremes of luxury and austerity. (I. 136)

To the Yogi everything is bliss. (I. 264-65)

The strong, the well-knit, the young, the healthy, the daring alone are fit to be Yogis. (I. 264)